GW01081147

A quarterly journal of socialist theory

Summer 2003
Contents

INTERNATIONAL SOCIALISM ★

A quarterly journal of socialist theory

IMPERIALISM HAS been the word on the lips of millions in the last two war-filled years. But there is disagreement as to what it really means: is waging war only of benefit to the arms manufacturers and the multinationals gaining lucrative contracts to rebuild war-ravaged countries? Or does it run deeper than that, to the heart of the logic of capitalism? Chris Harman, author of *A People's History of the World*, takes us through the bloody 20th century. He shows how a clear understanding of the relationship between military and economic competition is crucial for building an effective anti-imperialist movement today.

THE IRAQI PEOPLE are portrayed on our TV screens as victims—first of Saddam Hussein, then of US and UK bombs. Anne Alexander reveals the mass movements that shook Iraq in the 1940s and 1950s, when millions of workers and peasants rose up against imperialism.

MIKE KIDRON, who died recently, was the founding editor of this journal 43 years ago. Ian Birchall introduces a selection of extracts from his early editorials, spanning, among other things, pacifism and the bomb, confronting Nazis on our streets, and the role of the theoretical journal. Plus Brian Manning draws out the legacy of Marxist historian Christopher Hill.

ITALY, 1922, was a country on a knife-edge. We reprint an article first published in 1932 recounting how the people of Parma turned their streets into barricades, successfully fighting off Mussolini's 'punitive raids' and sending the fascists running with their tails between their legs. Book reviews include the young Marx and the anti-capitalist manifesto *Change the World Without Taking Power*.

Editor: John Rees. Assistant editors: Alex Callinicos, Chris Harman, John Molyneux, Lindsey German, Colin Sparks, Mike Gonzalez, Peter Morgan, Mike Haynes, Judy Cox, Jim Wolfreys, Sally Campbell, Megan Trudell, Mark O'Brien, Michael Lavalette, Sam Ashman and Rob Hoveman.

Issue 99 of INTERNATIONAL SOCIALISM, quarterly journal of the Socialist Workers Party (Britain)

Published July 2003
Copyright © International Socialism
Distribution/subscriptions: International Socialism,
PO Box 82, London E3 3LH
E-mail: isj@swp.org.uk
American distribution: B de Boer, 113 East Center Street, Nutley,
New Jersey 07110
US subscriptions: www.leftturnbooks.com
Editorial and production: 020 7538 5821
Sales and subscriptions: 020 7531 9810

ISBN 1 898876 06 1

Printed by BPC Wheatons Ltd, Exeter, England
Typeset by East End Offset, London E3
Cover by Sherborne Design Ltd

A full index for *International Socialism* is available at
www.lpi.org.uk
For details of back copies see the end pages of this book

Subscription rates for one year (four issues) are:

Britain and overseas (surface):	individual	£14 ($30)
	institutional	£25
Air speeded supplement:	North America	£2
	Europe/South America	£2
	elsewhere	£4

Note to contributors
The deadline for articles intended for issue 101 of
International Socialism is 1 September 2003.

All contributions should be double spaced with wide margins.
Please submit two copies. If you write your contribution
using a computer, please also supply a disk, together with
details of the computer and program used.

Analysing imperialism

CHRIS HARMAN

The US assault against Iraq has seen protests in virtually every major city in the world, not merely for peace, but against 'imperialism'. The word has been used by the unlikeliest of people to express their abhorrence at US government actions.

But there is not always clarity as to what imperialism means at the beginning of the 21st century. To some it represents the culmination of the development of capitalism over the last two and half centuries—the 'highest stage' of the system. To some it represents simply a grab for profitable raw materials or investment which the system as a whole could manage without, or a drive to increase the profits of just one section of the US ruling class, the military-industrial complex. There are even some who hold that states trying to conquer other states is an archaic practice followed by certain political leaders in contradiction to the dynamics of the system as whole. So Michael Hardt, co-author of the highly influential *Empire*, writes that 'the US is fast becoming an imperialist power along the old European model, but on a global scale', but hastens to add that 'business leaders around the globe recognise that imperialism is bad for business because it sets up barriers that hinder global flows'.[1] And Bernard Cassen, the leader of ATTAC in France and a key figure in the World Social Forum, claimed shortly before the attack on Iraq, 'Whether war breaks out or not, B-52s and special forces will not alter poverty in Brazil or hunger in Argentina'.[2]

The disagreements were between people who were agreed in resisting the latest act of aggression by the world's most powerful—and most

dangerous—state. But they remain important in determining how we
fight back in the long term. If imperialism is merely a set of state actions
cut off from the wider dynamic of the system, then pressures to reform
the state can bring peace. It is even possible to see the drive to war as
something standing in opposition to the wider trend of the system—
whether you call this, as apologists for the system do, 'free trade', or as
some opponents do, 'empire'. By contrast, if it is organically linked to
the system as a whole, you have to overthrow the system to remove the
threat.

Part 1: Classic theories of imperialism

The best known statement about the centrality of imperialism to the system
is Lenin's pamphlet *Imperialism: The Highest Stage of Capitalism*. It was
written in the midst of the First World War. Its aim was to be a 'popular
outline', showing how the resort to war was a product of the 'latest stage of
capitalism'—the original subtitle to the work:

> *Capitalism has grown into a world system of colonial oppression and financial*
> *strangulation of the overwhelming majority of the people of the world by a*
> *handful of 'advanced' countries. And this 'booty' is shared by two or three*
> *world-dominating pirates (America, England, Japan), armed to the teeth who*
> *embroil the whole world in **their** war over the division of **their** booty.*[3]

The capitalist powers, he points out, have partitioned the world
between them on the basis of 'a calculation of the strength of the participants, their general economic, financial, military and other strength'.
But 'the relative strength of these participants is not changing uni-
formly, for under capitalism there cannot be an equal development of
different undertakings, trusts, branches of industry or countries'. A partition of the world that corresponded to the relative strength of the great
powers at one point no longer does so a couple of decades later. The
partitioning of the world gives way to struggles over the repartitioning
of the world:

> *Peaceful alliances prepared the ground for wars and in their turn grow out of*
> *wars. One is the condition for the other, giving rise to alternating forms of*
> *peaceful and non-peaceful struggle **on one and the same basis**, that of impe-*
> *rialist connections and interrelations of world economics and world politics.*[4]

Lenin's theory was not just a theory of military conflicts between the
great powers. He insisted these conflicts were a product of changes in
capitalism itself:

Half a century ago, when Marx was writing **Capital***, free competition appeared to the overwhelming majority of economists to be a 'natural law'... Marx had proved that free competition gives rise to the concentration of production, which, in turn, at a certain stage of development, leads to monopoly. Today, monopoly has become a fact... The rise of monopolies, as the result of the concentration of production, is a general and fundamental law of the present stage of development of capitalism... For Europe, the time when the new capitalism* **definitely** *superseded the old can be established with fair precision; it was the beginning of the 20th century.*[5]

This is something quite different from the old free competition between manufacturers, scattered and out of touch with one another, and producing for an unknown market. Concentration has reached the point at which it is possible to make an approximate estimate of all sources of raw materials (for example, the iron ore deposits) of a country and even, as we shall see, of several countries, or of the whole world. Not only are such estimates made, but these sources are captured by gigantic monopolist associations. An approximate estimate of the capacity of markets is also made, and the associations 'divide' them up amongst themselves by agreement. Skilled labour is monopolised, the best engineers are engaged; the means of transport are captured—railways in America, shipping companies in Europe and America.[6]

But once this stage is reached, competition between the giant corporations is no longer based simply—or even mainly—on the old purely market methods. Taking control of raw materials so that rivals cannot get them, blocking rivals' access to transport facilities, selling goods at a loss so as to drive rivals out of business, denying them access to credit, are all methods used: 'There is no longer a competitive struggle between small and large, between the technically developed and the technically backward. We see here the monopolists throttling all those who do not submit to the monopoly, to its yoke, to its dictation'.[7] 'Monopolies bring with them everywhere monopolist principles: the utilisation of "connections" for profitable deals takes the place of competition in the open market'.[8]

And central among the connections are those linking the monopolies based in a particular country to its state. Lenin quoted the experience of four major industries to justify this account—steel and zinc, oil, and the electrical and merchant shipping of Europe and North America. From these he concluded that the development of monopoly at home has its corollary in the use of state power to establish influence abroad. The competitive struggle between the monopolies became a struggle between their states to control different parts of the world:

The capitalists divide the world, not out of any particular malice, but because the degree of concentration which has been reached forces them to adopt this method in order to obtain profits. And they divide it 'in proportion to capital', 'in proportion to strength', because there cannot be any other method of division under commodity production and capitalism.[9]

*The epoch of the latest stage of capitalism shows us that certain relations between capitalist associations grow up, **based** on the economic division of the world; while parallel to and in connection with it, certain relations grow up between political alliances, between states, on the basis of the territorial division of the world, of the struggle for colonies, of the 'struggle for spheres of influence'.*[10]

This found expression in the division of the world into the great empires—the British, the French, the Russian, the Belgian and the Dutch, which divided most of Asia and Africa between them in Lenin's time. But Lenin was insistent that imperialism involved more than the division between the great powers of what we would today call the 'Third World'. He criticises Karl Kautsky for writing, 'Imperialism...consists in the striving of every industrial capitalist nation to bring under its control or to annex all large areas of *agrarian* territory, irrespective of what nations inhabit it'.[11] The imperialist division of the world, Lenin insisted, was increasingly centred on industrial areas: 'The characteristic feature of imperialism is precisely that it strives to annex *not only* agrarian territories, but even most highly industrialised regions (German appetite for Belgium; French appetite for Lorraine)'.[12]

Lenin's fellow Bolshevik, Bukharin—whose *Imperialism and World Economy* was written shortly before Lenin's work, but which appeared afterwards, with an introduction by Lenin—made the argument just as forcefully:

Where formerly many individually owned enterprises competed with each other, there appears the most stubborn competition between a few gigantic capitalist combines pursuing a complicated and, to a considerable degree, calculated policy. There finally comes a time when competition ceases in an entire branch of production... The centralisation process proceeds apace. Combines...in industry and banking...unite the entire 'national' production, which assumes the form of a company of companies, thus becoming a state capitalist trust. Competition reaches its highest, the last conceivable, stage of development. It is now competition of the state capitalist trusts on the world market... Competition is reduced to a minimum within the boundaries of the 'national' economies, only to flare up in colossal proportions, such as would not have been possible in any of the preceding historical epochs... The centre of gravity is shifted in the com-

petition of gigantic, consolidated and organised economic bodies possessed of a colossal fighting capacity in the world tournament of 'nations'... Imperialist annexation is only a case of the general application of the general capitalist tendency towards centralisation of capital...

One may distinguish two sorts of centralisation: the one where an economic unit absorbs another unit of the same kind, and the one which we term vertical centralisation, where an economic unit absorbs another of a different kind... An example of horizontal imperialist annexation is the seizure of Belgium by Germany [in the First World War]; *an example of the vertical annexation is the seizure of Egypt by England... It is customary to reduce imperialism to colonial conquests alone... Now, however, the time has come for a fundamental redivision... Even the territory of the home country is drawn into the process of redivision.*[13]

Lenin and Bukharin's works were produced in the middle of the First World War, and their aim was to explain the forces behind it. Their enduring power lies in the way in which they still provide an explanation, like no other, of the whole of what has been called the '30 years war' of the 20th century—the great military clashes that tore Europe apart, causing a total of 50 million deaths and devastation all the way from the channel to the Volga, and sucking into the maelstrom hundreds of millions of people in the most distant stretches of the world. It was an explanation that spurred opponents of war in Europe and North America to challenge not merely the militarists, but also the economic system as a whole. And it spurred a whole generation of people fighting to shake off the shackles of empire in the Third World to see some sort of identity of interest with the workers' movements of the advanced countries.

The attacks on the theory

The sheer power of this theory of imperialism has led to repeated attempts to refute it. Since Bukharin became a non-person during the high tide of Stalinism,[14] most of the attacks—and defences—have been directed at Lenin's pamphlet.

The attacks have generally concentrated on two interlinked fronts. They have denied any empirical link between the great expansion of the Western colonial empires and the dynamics of capitalism. And they have argued that peaceful free trade rather than a militaristic struggle to control chunks of territory is the most profitable course for the majority of capitalists to pursue.

The first argument is not difficult to deal with. The great period of growth of the Western empires was the last quarter of the 19th century. Some European powers (Britain, Holland, France) already had empires, inherited from a previous phase of capitalist development, but not until the 1880s did they seek to divide all the world between them. In 1876 no more than 10 percent of Africa was under European rule. By 1900 more than 90 percent was colonised. In the same period Britain, France, Russia and Germany established wide spheres of influence extending out from colonial enclaves in China; Japan took over Korea and Taiwan; France conquered all of Indochina; the US seized Puerto Rico and the Philippines from Spain; and Britain and Russia agreed to an informal partitioning of Iran.

This was the period in which the export of capital became a central feature of the economy of Britain, still the world's dominant capitalist country. Total investment in foreign stocks rose from £95 million in 1883 to £393 million in 1889. It soon equalled 8 percent of Britain's gross national product and absorbed 50 percent of savings.[15] Its biggest colony, India, accounted for 12 percent of its exports of goods and 11 percent of its capital exports, while providing a surplus to Britain's balance of payments that could help pay for investments elsewhere in the world.[16] At the same time, many of the raw materials required for the most technologically advanced industries of the time came from colonial areas (vegetable oils for margarine and soap manufacture, copper for the electrical industry, rubber and oil for the fledgeling automobile industry).

The 1870s and early 1880s had been a period of depressed markets, falling prices, and low profits and dividends in Britain. With the growth of foreign investment this 'great depression' came to an end.[17]

It is not true that the exports of capital, let alone of goods, went to the colonies. Much went to the US, and quite a lot went to Latin American countries like Argentina. But what mattered for both politicians and industrial interests was that 'Britain ruled the waves'. There was a global empire, in which direct dominance in some parts of the world contributed to hegemony—and defence of economic interests—in other areas.

As I have put the argument elsewhere:

Colonies offered the capitalists of the colonial power protected outlets for investment. They also provided military bases to protect routes to investment elsewhere. For Britain possessions such as Malta, Cyprus, Egypt, South Yemen and the Cape were important not just as sources of profit in their own right, but as stopping-off places to India—and India, 'the jewel in the crown', was also a stopping-off place to Singapore, the tin and rubber of Malaya, the recently opened markets of China, and the rich dominions of Australia and New Zealand. The empire was like a woven garment which stopped British capitalism catching a cold: a single thread might seem of little importance, but if snapped the rest would start unravelling. At least that was how those who ran the empire, their colleagues in the City of London and their friends in British industry saw things.[18]

Where British capitalism went, others wanted to follow and set about grabbing what they could. It was usually a case of first come, first served. France took huge swathes of North and West Africa, Belgium's king seized a vast area of the Congo region, and the Dutch consolidated their scattered holdings in the East Indies into a modern empire. But the one country in Europe that was beginning to overtake British capitalism industrially, Germany, was the last to join the race, only getting Tanganyika (the main part of modern Tanzania), South West Africa (Namibia), Cameroon, Togo and Rwanda-Burundi as consolation prizes. By the turn of the century there were powerful voices in German industry connected to the National Liberal Party (after 1918 the National People's Party) who were arguing that German business could only compete globally if Germany had more colonies—or at least a sphere of influence stretching through eastern and south eastern Europe.

Whichever way you look at the 1890s and the 1900s—or for that matter the 1920s and the 1930s—you find that empire was seen as a positive economic advantage by capitalist classes. There would be differences of opinion over the advantages to be gained from particular imperialist adventures. There was no great divergence about the benefits of empire in general.

But this still leaves open the second objection. Was it really in the interests of businessmen to see their taxes burnt up in wars that disrupted markets? Would it not have been preferable for them to have forced through policies based on free trade and peaceful competition for markets, pushing aside those narrow interests which benefited directly from arms spending and colonies?

This was essentially the argument of one of the first accounts of imperialism, produced by the English liberal economist Hobson, whose work was published in 1902. He saw imperialism as the product of one interest group, those connected with certain financial institutions. These opted for guaranteed returns of interest on overseas loans rather than taking the risks involved in industrial investment at home, and welcomed colonial expansion as a way of making sure their state guaranteed the safety of their investments:

> *Seeing that the imperialism of the last three decades is clearly condemned as a business policy, in that at enormous expense it has procured a small, bad, unsafe increase of markets, and has jeopardised the entire wealth of the nation in rousing the strong resentment of other nations, we may ask, 'How is the British nation induced to embark upon such unsound business?' The only possible answer is that the business interests of the nation as a whole are subordinated to those of certain sectional interests that usurp control of the national resources and use them for their private gain.*[19]

He identifies these as being the arms manufacturers, 'the great manufacturers for export trade', 'the shipping trade', but insists that 'by far the
most important economic factor in imperialism is the influence relating to
investments... The period of energetic imperialism has been coincident
with a remarkable growth in the income from external investments... To a
larger extent every year Great Britain is becoming a nation living upon
tribute from abroad, and the classes who enjoy this tribute have an ever-
increasing incentive to employ the public policy, the public purse and the
public force to extend the field of their private investments, and to safe-
guard and improve their existing investments.'
So one small section of the capitalist class has, in effect, turned the
state to its own advantage, despite the harm it does to the rest:

*Aggressive imperialism, which costs the taxpayer so dear, which is of so little
value to the manufacturer and trader, which is fraught with such grave incal-
culable peril to the citizen, is a source of great gain to the investor who
cannot find at home the profitable use he seeks for his capital, and insists that
his government should help him to profitable and secure investments abroad.*

This includes a layer of *rentiers*—bond holders who receive their dividends regularly without ever having to worry themselves with
productive or commercial activity of any sort. But at the centre of it is
something 'still more dangerous'—'the special interest of the financier,
the general dealer in investments...the great financial houses, who use
stocks and shares not so much as investments to yield them interest, but
as material for speculation in the money market'.
He adds, in a passage that shows hostility to 'finance' rather than
capitalism as a whole, which has the potential to lead in a dangerous
direction:

*United by the strongest bonds of organisation, always in closest and
quickest touch with one another, situated in the very heart of the business
capital of every state, controlled, so far as Europe is concerned, chiefly by
men of a single and peculiar race, who have behind them many centuries of
financial experience, they are in a unique position to control the policy of
nations.*[20]

The alternative to imperialism, on Hobson's reasoning, was not the
revolutionary overthrow of capitalism, but governmental action to expand
the domestic economy and defend the interests of industry against
finance. Such action would form the basis of an alliance uniting trade
unions and the great majority of business interests in opposition to the
rentiers and the finance capitalists.

Ten years later Karl Kautsky, the veteran theorist of the German Social Democratic Party, came up with a very similar account of imperialism. The political biography by Massimo Salvadori summarises his view:

> *In the past several years finance capitalism had come to the forefront of the internal and international scene. The finance capitalists, who drew their profits from the export of capital, represented the most reactionary and militaristic force in domestic politics, since they had a direct interest in transforming each national state into an apparatus of support for their own expansion. Imperialism was therefore directly linked to finance capitalism. But the interests of finance capital were not identical to those of industrial capital, which could expand only by broadening its markets through free trade. It was from the industrial sector that impulses towards international concord arose in the bourgeois camp. It was with this sector that social democracy should link up to safeguard peace. Imperialism, the expression of one phase of capitalist development and the cause of armed conflicts, was not the only possible form of development of capitalism.*[21]

Along with finance capitalists, Kautsky also saw the arms producers as having an interest in imperialism and war. But he maintained that 'the economic costs of rearmament, while they favoured the development of some sectors of industry, were detriments to others'.[22] 'The source of the political power of finance capital, which aimed at subjugating all society, could be traced back to its union with militarism and the bureaucracy'.[23]

From his view that capitalism as whole had no interest in partitioning the world into rival colonies, Kautsky drew the conclusion that it was approaching a new stage. He developed this argument in an article he wrote in 1914 in which he saw the colonisation of the previous three decades as a result of industrial capitalists trying to secure for themselves raw materials and markets.

'Capitalist accumulation in industry can proceed freely only when the agricultural region which supplies its raw material and consumes its products is constantly being enlarged.' There were various ways to do this. One was called 'imperialism', especially fostered by the system of investing capital in agrarian countries which encouraged 'efforts to reduce these lands to a state of political dependence'. 'The effort to subdue and hold agrarian regions' had caused serious conflicts between the great capitalist powers which led to 'tremendous competition in armaments' and 'long-prophesied world war'.

But, he went on to argue, 'this phase of imperialism' was not necessary to the continued existence of capitalism:

There is no economic necessity for the continuation of the great competition in the production of armaments after the close of the present war. At best such a continuation would serve the interests of only a few capitalist groups. On the contrary capitalist industry is threatened by the conflicts between the various governments. Every far-sighted capitalist must call out to his associates: Capitalists of all lands unite! From a purely economic point of view, therefore, it is not impossible that capitalism is now to enter upon a new phase, a phase marked by the transfer of trust methods to international politics, a sort of super-imperialism.[24]

Monopolies, the state and finance capital

Lenin's *Imperialism* is very much a critique of Kautsky. It rests on three planks.

First, there is the argument that the whole system is in a monopoly stage. Monopolies are not just, as are Hobson's financiers or Kautsky's finance capitalists, individual elements within each national economy. They are the central, dominating forms of capital, dragging other sections behind them.

Second, in such a situation the political 'influence' they exert is not an accidental feature. It is intrinsic to the form capitalist competition now takes. No large capital can survive unless it has connections to the state and uses these to expand at the expense of other capitals. Or, to put the argument another way, capitalism is never simply an abstract system of free flowing capital. The system has always been composed of different individual capitals, each run by people who attempt to use their connections with each other and with the state to cheat the market. But under the 'free market' capitalism of Marx's time, none was big enough to influence the dynamic of the system as a whole. By contrast, in Lenin's picture individual capitals dominate each major sector of production within each country and are able, through their connections with each other and the state, to impose a whole new dynamic of political and military expansionism on society as a whole.

Finally, Lenin backs up his points by his empirical accounts of the development of major industrial concerns. It is his ability to marshal such arguments and facts that enables Lenin to insist so convincingly that any agreement between the great capitalist powers at the end of the First World War will give way to new conflict and renewed war.

There are, however, certain subsidiary problems with the way Lenin presents his arguments that leave a back door open for arguments of the Kautsky sort.

In his pamphlet Lenin readily acknowledges his use of Hobson's work and that of the Austrian Marxist economist Hilferding, who was also an important influence on Kautsky's views on imperialism.[25] Lenin is critical of both. But he puts at the very centre of his analysis Hilferding's use of the phrase 'finance capital' to describe the dominant feature of the system in its imperialist phase, and he accepts much of Hobson's description of the dominant and parasitic role of finance within this.

Hilferding had carried through a very important account of the changes in capitalism in the quarter of a century after Marx's death in 1883—the rise of the joint stock company in place of the individual entrepreneur, the growing importance of the banks as a source of investment, and the role of the state in protecting the markets of already mature national capitalisms. There was, he argued, a merging together of financial capital and industrial capital to produce a synthesis of the two.

But there was a central ambiguity in Hilferding's own use of 'finance capital'. At some points it meant a merger of finance and industry—or at least financial interests lubricating the merger of industrial concerns: 'The banks have to invest an ever-increasing part of their capital in industry, and in this way they become to a greater and greater extent industrial capitalists. I call bank capital...which is actually transformed in this way into industrial capital, finance capital'.[26] 'Industry becomes increasingly dependent upon bank capital, but this does not mean that the magnates of industry also become dependent on banking magnates'.[27]

On this basis giant trusts and cartels were emerging that could dominate whole sectors of industry. They leaned on the state to protect their domestic markets, so enabling them to raise their prices at home—and attempt to conquer foreign markets with lower prices. It was this pressure of the combined finance-industrial capitals that changed the whole attitude of capital to the state. 'It is not free trade England, but the protectionist countries, Germany and the United States, which become the models of capitalist development,' wrote Hilferding.[28] Far from continuing with the traditional liberal notion of a minimal 'night-watchman state', the great trusts wanted a state with the power to widen its boundaries so as to enlarge the market in which they could gain monopoly profits: 'While free trade was indifferent to colonies, protectionism leads directly to a more active colonial policy, and to conflicts of interest between different states'.[29] The drive for empire was endemic in the most modern forms of capitalism. And since British, French and, to a lesser degree, Dutch and Belgian capitalism had already carved the world up between them, the expansion of German capitalism inevitably meant military clashes with them.

But Hilferding also used the term 'finance capital' in a way resonant of Hobson's description of finance as something with interests in opposition to those of the mass of industrial capitals:

> *The mobilisation of capital and the continual expansion of credit gradually bring about a complete change in the position of the money capitalists. The power of the banks increases, and they become the founders and eventually the rulers of industry, whose profits they seize for themselves as finance capital, just as formerly the old usurer seized, in the form of 'interest', the produce of the peasants and the ground rent of the lord of the manor.*[30]

The finance capitalists were then seen as the force pushing for colonies and wars, even while the industrial capitalists want to hold back. In a review Kautsky paraphrased Hilferding as calling finance capital 'the most brutal and violent form of capital'.[31]

But the ambiguity in Hilferding's formulation enabled him to draw a directly contradictory conclusion and so say that the rise of finance capital has an ameliorative impact on the rest of the system, by bringing about a growing organisation of the national economy, making it less subject to slumps, booms and market frenzies: 'The mass psychoses which speculation generated at the beginning of the capitalist era…seem gone forever'.[32] Within a few years Hilferding was developing this into a whole theory of 'organised capitalism', supposedly on its way to banishing major economic crises and the inevitable drive towards war forever.[33]

The use of the term 'finance capital' can still lead to such confusions today. Those who preach very limited reforms of the present system, like Will Hutton, blame the problems of British capitalism on the political dominance of City of London financiers, while a section of the anti-globalisation movement see a 'Tobin tax' directed against the cross-border financial flows as the way to deal with economic crises and world poverty.

Lenin was scathing about the trend in Hilferding's politics, describing him as an 'ex-Marxist'.[34] But he took over the term finance capital and puts it at the centre of his own theory. In doing so he left his own work open to ambiguous interpretations. His intention was to insist that the tendency towards monopoly meant that the core capitals in each country were driven to imperialist policies of dividing and redividing the world. For this reason, he criticised one of Hilferding's definitions of 'finance capital' as 'capital controlled by banks and employed by industrialists' as 'incomplete':

> *It is silent on one extremely important fact: the increase of concentration of production and of capital to such an extent that concentration leads, and has led, to monopoly… The concentration of production; the monopolies arising therefrom; the merging or coalescence of the banks with industry—such is the history of the rise of finance capital and such is the content of this term.*[35]

But the phraseology of certain other parts of the pamphlet has allowed people to interpret him as saying, rather as Hobson and Kautsky did, that financial interests and the banks were mainly responsible for imperialism. This was especially so when, basing himself on Hobson, he insisted on the 'parasitic' character of finance capital, writing of 'the extraordinary growth of a class, or rather of a social stratum of *rentiers*, ie people who live by "clipping coupons", who take no part in any enterprise whatever, whose profession is idleness. The export of capital, one of the most essential economic bases of imperialism, still more completely isolates the *rentiers* from production, and sets the seal of parasitism on the whole country that lives by exploiting the labour of several overseas countries and colonies'.[36] This stress on the 'parasitism' of finance capital allowed some people who supposedly based themselves on his work to claim in the decades after his death that it was possible to form anti-imperialist alliances with sections of industrial capital against finance capital—that is, to fall back precisely into the Kautsky policy that Lenin attacked so bitterly.

It also seemed to make the whole theory of imperialism rest upon the key role of the banks in exporting financial capital. But this did not fit with the picture even when Lenin was writing, let alone in the decades afterwards. The export of finance—and of the *rentiers*—was a central feature of *British* capitalism in the two decades before Hobson wrote. But Britain no longer 'showed the future' to other capitalist countries, as it had in Marx's day. Its new competitors, like Germany and the US, had leapt over Britain when it came to the concentration and monopolisation of industry. In the German case it was the industrial combines, especially those in heavy industry, that sought to expand beyond national frontiers by the establishment of colonies and spheres of influence. Moreover, the characteristic feature of the US and Russian economies in this period was not the export of capital but the inflow of funds from other capitalist countries (although here there was some re-export of capital). On a strict reading of Lenin's *Imperialism* these would seem not to be imperialist states at all at the time of the First World War, even though both had joined in the partitioning of the rest of the world in the previous quarter of a century.

This focus on financiers is even more problematic when we come to the quarter of a century *after* Lenin wrote. Britain began to go down the German road with the formation of its own great industrial near-monopolies (ICI, Unilever, etc), while it was heavy industry that played the key part in pushing the redivision of Europe in Germany's interests in the 1930s. And, as Tony Cliff pointed out, Japanese imperialism followed a policy of industrialising parts of its Taiwanese, Korean and Manchurian colonies as an extension of its own economy.[37] Overall Cliff noted, 'While in the years 1860 to 1914 the quantity of capital invested abroad by the advanced capitalist countries grew almost uninterruptedly, from 1914, by when imperialism had reached maturity, the quantity of capital invested abroad never rose above the level of 1914 and even declined below it'.[38]

What is more, far from the imperialist powers becoming deindustri-alised parasites living to an ever increasing extent off incomes obtained from production elsewhere in the world, they experienced the expansion of new industries in the years between the wars, which increased the gap between them and most of the rest of the world. Yet they also remained intent on imperialist expansion, with Britain and France grabbing most of the Middle East and the former German colonies, Japan expanding into China, and Germany then beginning to carve out a new empire in Europe.

Lenin, by leaning excessively on Hobson's interpretation of Britain before 1900, damages his own argument.

Bukharin and the drive to war

Bukharin's account of imperialism holds up much better, despite being much less widely known. He uses the category of 'finance capital' repeat-edly in *Imperialism and World Economy*. But he explicitly warns against seeing it as something distinct from industrial capital.

'Finance capital...must not be confused with money capital, for finance capital is characterised by being simultaneously banking *and* industrial capital'.[39] It is inseparable, for Bukharin, from the trend towards domination of the whole national economy by 'state capitalist trusts':

> The individual production branches are in various ways knit together into one collective body, organised on a large scale. Finance capital seizes the entire country in an iron grip. 'National economy' turns into one gigantic combined trust whose partners are the financial groups and the state. Such formations we call state capitalist trusts.[40]

The export of capital to satisfy the desire of *rentiers* is only one sub-ordinate feature of a system in which giant industrial firms increasingly linked to the state struggle with each other in international competition. This competition takes place on three different fronts—for commodity exports, for raw material and for capital exports: 'Those three roots of the policy of finance capitalism, however, represent in substance only three facets of the same phenomenon, namely of the conflict between the growth of productive forces on the one hand, and the "national" limits of the production organisation on the other'.[41]

In his later *Economics of the Transformation Period,* Bukharin sug-gests that 'finance capitalism' tends towards a new imperialist stage of capitalism, state capitalism:

*The state organisation of the bourgeoisie concentrated within itself the entire power of this class. Consequently, all remaining organisations...must be subordinated to the state. All are 'militarised'... Thus there arises a new model of state power, the classical model of the **imperialist** state, which relies on **state capitalist** relations of production. Here 'economics' is organisationally fused with 'politics'; the economic power of the bourgeoisie unites itself directly with the political power; the state ceases to be a simple protector of the process of exploitation and becomes a direct, capitalist collective exploiter...*

State capitalist relations of production are, logically and historically, a continuation of finance capitalist relations and constitute the completion of the latter. It is therefore not surprising that the starting point of their development constituted those organisational forms that were given by finance capital, ie syndicates, trusts and banks.[42]

Once this stage is reached 'there is a struggle of economies against each other, a war of capitalist competition. The form of this competition can be widely different. The imperialist policy...is one form of this competition.'

War now becomes central to the system, arising from the competition between the 'state capitalist trusts', but also feeding back into and determining their internal organisation:

With the formation of state capitalist trusts, competition is being almost entirely shifted to foreign countries; obviously, the organs of the struggle that is to be waged abroad, primarily state power, must therefore grow tremendously... Whenever a question arises about changing commercial treaties, the state power of the contracting groups of capitalists appears on the scene, and the mutual relations of those states—reduced in the final analysis to the relations between their military forces—determine the treaty. When a loan is to be granted to one or the other country, the government, basing itself on military power, secures the highest possible rate of interest for its nationals, guarantees obligatory orders, stipulates concessions, struggles against foreign competitors. When the struggle begins for the exploitation by finance capital of a territory that has not been formally occupied by anybody, again the military power of the state decides who will possess that territory. In 'peaceful' times the military state apparatus is hidden behind the scenes where it never stops functioning; in war times it appears on the scene most directly...

If state power is generally growing in significance, the growth of its military organisation, the army and the navy, is particularly striking. The struggle between state capitalist trusts is decided in the first place by the relation between their military forces, for the military power of the country is the last resort of the struggling 'national' groups of capitalists. The immensely growing state budget devotes an ever larger share to 'defence purposes', as militarisation is euphemistically termed...

Every improvement in military technique entails a reorganisation and reconstruction of the military mechanism; every innovation, every expansion of the military power of one state, stimulates all the others. What we observe here is like the phenomenon we come across in the sphere of tariff policies where a raise of rates in one state is immediately reflected in all others, causing a general raise...

Capitalist society is unthinkable without armaments, as it is unthinkable without wars. And just as it is true that not low prices cause competition but, on the contrary, competition causes low prices, it is equally true that not the existence of arms is the prime cause and the moving force in wars (although wars are obviously impossible without arms) but, on the contrary, the inevitableness of economic conflicts conditions the existence of arms. This is why in our times, when economic conflicts have reached an unusual degree of intensity, we are witnessing a mad orgy of armaments.[43]

Speaking in 1922, he argued:

The main groups of the bourgeoisie are now of the nature of trustified groups within the framework of the state... It is quite conceivable that such a form of enterprise should resort chiefly to violent forms of competition... Thus arise the new forms of competition which lead to military attack by the state.[44]

Bukharin here foreshadows the version of imperialism that characterised the late 1930s and the 1940s. But in one respect he was weaker than Lenin—in terms of drawing the political consequence of his theory when it came to the countries oppressed by imperialism.

Lenin, imperialism and the colonial countries

Imperialism: The Highest Stage of Capitalism had had an enormous impact on the colonial liberation movements—and on those showing solidarity with them in the imperialist countries. This was partly because it was a clear call for workers within imperialist countries to oppose the policies of their own rulers. It was also because it was read in association with other writings by him on the right of peoples to self determination.

In these Lenin had dealt with the *political* implications of imperialism. He saw that the revolt of the oppressed nationalities within the great empires that dominated the world could tear them apart. These revolts could arouse much wider layers of the population to action and weaken the Western capitalist states running the great empires—and this was true even if the revolts were led by remnants of the old pre-capitalist exploiting classes or by the newly emerging bourgeois groups. What mattered was that these local exploiting classes were politically dominated by the states of the great empires, and in fighting back weakened those states. Revolutionary socialists had to encourage and aid such fightbacks by unconditionally supporting the right of political self determination in the face of imperialist oppression.

Lenin was criticised in the years before 1917 by other revolutionaries, such as Rosa Luxemburg, Pyatakov and Bukharin. They said that political independence under the leadership of such exploiting groups would be meaningless, since they would still be economically dependent upon the more powerful imperialist ruling classes within a world capitalist system.

This was neither here nor there for Lenin. The struggle for national self determination was a political struggle, directed against concrete oppressive political institutions, the world's most powerful states.

He spelt this out strongly after the Dublin rising against British rule in 1916:

> To imagine that social revolution is **conceivable** without revolts by small nations in the colonies and in Europe, without revolutionary outbursts by a section of the petty bourgeoisie **with all its prejudices**, without a movement of the politically non-conscious proletarian and semi-proletarian masses, against oppression by the landowners, the church, and the monarchy, against national oppression, etc—to imagine all this is to **repudiate social revolution**. So one army lines up in one place and says, 'We are for socialism,' and another somewhere else and says, 'We are for imperialism,' and that will be a social revolution! Only those who hold such a ridiculously pedantic view could vilify the Irish rebellion by calling it a 'putsch'. Whoever expects a 'pure' social revolution will **never** live to see it. Such a person pays lip-service to revolution without understanding what revolution is.[45]

He was insistent on the difference between political independence and economic independence. One was achievable through political struggle, and the other was a utopian demand once capitalism had established a world market, so making production in any one state, even the most powerful, dependent on production elsewhere.

But the potential forces for *political* struggle were enormous. Lenin prophesied rebellions for the rights of oppressed nationalities within all of the great empires—and his prophecy proved correct in the years after 1916 when such rebellions took off in Ireland, India, Egypt and Indonesia, and against the European and Japanese 'concessions' in China. And his insistence that the workers' parties on the left had unconditionally to support such rebellions attracted towards the newly formed Communist International a number of important activists from the colonial movements.[46] By the mid-1920s Communist advisers were playing a key role in nationalist armies fighting for control of southern China, and over the next three decades Communists provided with a bowdlerised version of Lenin's theory by Stalin were able to influence some important national liberation movements in the colonial world (although, they could lose such influence when, as in during the Quit India movement of 1942, Stalin's influence led them to oppose national liberation struggles).

But there was one big problem with Lenin's theory when it came to the colonial world. *Imperialism: The Highest Stage of Capitalism* held that the export of capital to the colonies would lead to their industrial development:

> *The export of capital influences and greatly accelerates the development of capitalism in those countries to which it is exported. While, therefore, the export of capital may tend to a certain extent to arrest development in the capital-exporting countries, it can only do so by expanding and deepening the further development of capitalism throughout the world.*[47]

One of Lenin's earliest works, *The Development of Capitalism in Russia*, had been directed against those who denied the possibility of capitalist development. He continued to stand by this position when he wrote *Imperialism*. It was this belief that industrial development was increasingly in the colonies that led him to describe the colonising countries as 'parasitic'.[48]

However, the attraction of Communism to many in the national liberation movements had been because of the perception that capitalism was *not* producing appreciable industrial advance. In many Third World countries there was a very large urban middle class which suffered from impoverishment, precarious job opportunities and unemployment, as well as political marginalisation by the colonial set-up. The lack of willingness of movements dependent on the local bourgeoisie to wage a consistent and determined struggle against colonialism could attract some of the urban middle class to Communism—provided Communism addressed their concerns about economic development as well as political independence. A debate over this issue arose in the Communist International in 1927-1928, just before complete Stalinisation destroyed any possibility of rational debate within it.

Jane Degras has written:

> *The chief point in dispute was whether the colonies were being 'decolonised', ie whether the metropolitan countries were promoting or retarding the industrialisation of their colonies; India served as the focus of this discussion... Members of the British delegation believed Britain was industrialising India*

to take advantage of cheap labour there. Bukharin in his introductory speech came out against the decolonisation theory; the Indians themselves were divided; Roy…had written that decolonisation was proceeding and contained the seeds of the dissolution of the British Empire. He is said to have advanced the decolonisation theory at the end of 1927. The bourgeoisie were not only withdrawing from the national revolution, but were moving towards an agreement with the imperialists to contain it. S Tagore (appearing under the name Narayan) claims that…in April 1927 he and Bukharin agreed that some sort of decolonisation was proceeding in India.[49]

Kuusinen, Stalin's man in the Comintern at the time, then intervened to insist, 'If it were true that British imperialism had really turned to the industrialisation of India, we should have to revise our entire conception of the nature of imperialist colonial policy'[50]—without, of course, recognising that any 'revision' would have meant agreeing with Lenin's writings! He then went on to claim, 'Investment was not industrialisation… Britain was determined to destroy the industry of India and thrust the proletariat back into the villages; it has found its agent in Gandhi.'

Two British delegates, Arnot and Rothstein, argued back, 'Imperialism by its own contradictions fostered industrial development in the colonies that was going to compete with it, thus transferring domestic contradictions onto the world scene'.[51] But the theses of the Congress were adamant: 'There is an objective impossibility of a non-capitalist path of development for the backward countries… The specific colonial forms of capitalist exploitation…hinder the development of the productive forces of the colonies'.[52] This argument became cast in stone during the following decades of Stalinism, when it was used to argue that the only way colonial and ex-colonial countries could develop economically was to follow the pattern established in the USSR.

There was a convergence between this current of ideas rooted in the Stalinist tradition with another current that had arisen, more or less independently, in Latin America. Direct colonial rule had ended in most of the region in the 1820s. But in the first decades of the 20th century the conditions of life of people in large areas of it were hardly different to those for the colonised peoples of Africa and Asia. There were impoverished peasantries, urban bourgeoisies unable fully to wrest power from landed oligarchies, and a large, educated petty bourgeoisie which resented its inability to achieve lifestyles like those that existed in North America and Western Europe.

Movements began to arise in the inter-war years that saw the main obstacle to economic advance as lying in the stultifying influence of British and American imperialism. Haya de la Torre, son of an unsuccessful businessman, formed the Alianza Revolucionaria Peruana (APRA) in 1924 around a programme of nationalism and anti-imperialism which gathered wide support from both the middle class and workers in Peru, and encouraged middle class activists in other countries to follow suit: 'For at least 20 years, from 1930 to 1950, Haya de la Torre was the anti-imperialist guide of a whole generation of enlightened bourgeois and even of the proletariat'.[53]

The crisis of the early 1930s hit the Latin American economies—and their ruling classes—very hard. From 1900 to 1930 they had, if anything, gained slightly from trends in world trade.[54] Now they saw the price of their exports collapse. As economic crisis turned to political crisis, sections emerged within the ruling class who formed blocs with sections of the middle class, and in some cases certain leaders of the labour movement, to push for an economic policy designed to shift resources from the production of raw materials and food to industrialisation.

As Roxborough writes:

> The theorists...argued there was an immediate and direct link between changes in the industrialised countries at the centre and the underdeveloped countries at the periphery. From the late 19th century until the middle of the 20th...Latin America had taken on the role of supplier of raw materials and foodstuffs to the industrialised nations and had, in return, imported manufactured products... They argued—and on this there is some controversy—that...the terms of trade had been moving against Latin American nations since about 1870. This meant that every quantum of Latin American exports brought in return a smaller and smaller quantum of imports of manufactured goods... The only realistic policy for Latin American countries to adopt was a deliberate policy of fostering...import substitution industrialisation... This meant an attack on the old landed exporting oligarchies by a process of land reform and export diversification, and a redistribution of income to increase consumer demand for relatively low priced manufactured goods...
>
> In political terms, the strategy was seen as an alliance of nearly all social classes against the landed oligarchy... In many ways this analysis was similar to the argument put forward by the Communist Party, which...argued that revolutionaries should support the 'progressive national bourgeoisie' in its struggle to remove the last vestiges of feudalism and imperialist domination, and modernise the economy.[55]

Governments like that of Vargas in Brazil and then that of Peron in Argentina moved strongly in the direction suggested by such arguments, but so did others, so that for a time the policy was virtually the orthodoxy. Such governments were not in any serious sense hostile to US or Western European capitalism. But their policies did face varying degrees of opposition from powerful landowning classes who had commercial and financial links with Britain or the US, and it was possible for the 'populist' politicians to give a nationalist and supposedly anti-imperialist tinge to their policies. Co-opting the APRA-type nationalism of the middle classes, they interpreted history before and after independence from Spain as being one of imperialist domination. This enabled them to get their way in pushing recalcitrant sections of capital into line, denouncing them as 'anti-national', while enjoying the support of other sections who stood to gain massively from industrialisation policies. It also enabled them to fragment the working class movement between those who, putting class interests first, denounced their domestic policies (and the governments as 'fascist', or at least 'semi-fascist'), and those who justified being co-opted by those governments on the grounds that they were 'fighting imperialism'.[56]

The Second World War: the confirmation of the theory

The Second World War was the great and barbaric confirmation of the classic theory of imperialism. Lenin and Bukharin had insisted, in opposition to people like Kautsky, that the great capitalist powers would be forced to move from peace to war as they strove to partition and repartition the world. And this is what happened in the mid to late 1930s in response to unprecedented economic crisis. Each national capitalism turned to a greater or lesser degree to an integration between national capital and the national state—and the other side of this 'state monopoly capitalism' was the use of 'protectionist' measures to restrict direct market competition from foreign capitalists. World trade, which had risen fourfold between 1891 and 1925, by 1932 had fallen back to the level of 1905. The imperialism of countries seeking to penetrate distant parts of the world through capital exports turned into the imperialism of countries trying to form tight trading blocs in opposition to each other. But capitalist states could not simply undo their dependence upon components and materials from outside their own borders. This put a greater premium than before on the national state being able to exert direct political influence to control resources beyond its own borders—to imperialism of one sort or another.

The result was a recurrence, on a more intense basis, of the tension that had culminated in the First World War. The established colonial powers, especially Britain and France, were able to rely upon their existing empires—enlarged by the seizure of German colonies and much of the Middle East in the aftermath of the First World War—to create political-economic blocs, dominated by their own currencies (known respectively as the sterling area and gold bloc). The US was able to increase its influence, particularly in Latin America, after buying up many British investments there during the First World War. The world's second industrial power, Germany, was restricted to an even narrower national territory than in 1914. It had lost its colonies, and

France had made a series of alliances in Eastern Europe (the 'Little Entente') directed at reducing German influence there, and even over German-speaking Austria. In the Far East expanding Japanese capitalism similarly felt penned in by the colonial rule exercised by the French over Vietnam, the British over Malaya, the Dutch over the East Indies (present day Indonesia) and the US over the Philippines—as well as by the continuing British and French 'concessions' in China.

The rulers of Germany and Japan went for political options that, as well as repression of the working class movement at home, subordinated individual capitalists to programmes of national capitalist accumulation imposed by the state. The Nazi government used dictatorial political powers to impose regimentation on the economy. The major capitalist groups remained intact. But from now on they were subordinated to the needs of an arms drive which they themselves supported. Armaments and the expansion of heavy industry drove the whole economy forward, providing markets and outlets for investment. However, there was one major problem with any such policy. Germany was not a self contained economic unit. The only way to overcome instability in raw material sources was to expand the boundaries of the German Reich so as to incorporate neighbouring economies, and to subordinate their industries to the German military drive. The logic of state-directed monopoly capitalism led to a form of imperialism Lenin had referred to in 1916 and which was central to Bukharin's theory—the seizure of 'highly industrialised regions'.[57] Beyond a certain point such expansion led to inevitable clashes with other great powers who feared threats to their own spheres of influence and empires. As they reacted by resorting to armed force, the German regime in turn had to direct even more of the economy towards arms—and reach out to grab new territory—in order 'defend' the lands it had already grabbed.

As I have written elsewhere:

Once the path of military expansion had been decided upon, it fed upon itself. To challenge the existing empires required the maximum military-industrial potential. Every successful imperialist adventure increased this—for example, the Japanese takeover of Manchuria, the German annexation of Austria and then Czechoslovakia. But at the same time it increased the hostility of the existing empires—leading to the need for a greater arms potential and further military adventures. The breaking points were the German seizure of western Poland and the Japanese onslaught on Pearl Harbour.[58]

The rulers of the existing French and British empire were driven to resist. Many were reluctant to do so with the experience of the previous world war in mind. They feared that the cost of another would eat up their already diminished foreign investments, they were terrified of a repetition of the revolutionary upheavals that had threatened 20 years before, and they saw the rapidly industrialising USSR as nearly as dangerous as their old German rival. They hoped that somehow a German imperialism controlling the core of north western and central Europe would be able to coexist with their own domination of vast tracts of Africa and Asia. But in the end they were forced to fight. For Britain and France what was involved was no longer a struggle to grab new sources of surplus value, but to hang on to what they already had. They had to fight together against German imperialism if their own imperialisms were not to suffer. Their alliance was joined in the summer of 1941 by Russia, once the logic of German expansion led it to move on from victory over Poland, Belgium and France to push into the Ukraine and south east towards the oil of Baku. A few months later the US was also forced into the war as the logic of Japanese imperialism led it to try to grab the poorly defended Far Eastern possessions of all the Western capitalisms.

The alliance against Germany and Japan overshadowed the clashes between the other imperialisms. In the 1920s there had been predictions of a major clash between the US and Britain both by some within the British Foreign Office and by Leon Trotsky. The predictions were not fulfilled. There were sharp clashes of interest between the British and US governments in the course of the Second World War. They jostled for influence over Saudi Arabia with its oilfields, and there was bitter resentment by British ministers like Eden over the way the US effectively made British capitalism liquidate overseas investments in order to pay its bills for US weapons and food.[59] But greater hostility to the demands of German and Japanese imperialism led to British imperialism accepting, grudgingly, a subordination to US interests.

Part 2: Imperialism in the Cold War years

The clash of imperialisms in the 1930s had taken the form of the conflict between Britain and France with their diffuse global empires and Germany as it built a continental empire in Europe. With the defeat of Germany, a new conflict in some ways similar grew up between the two great victors of the war.

The US had aspirations for its industries, the most advanced and productive in the world, to penetrate the whole world economy through 'free trade'. The Western European powers, exhausted by the war, were in no position to challenge it directly (although British politicians often expressed a private desire to be so). But the other victor, the USSR, was in such a position. Its ruling bureaucracy had embarked with a degree of success on the forced industrialisation of their country in the late 1920s by subordinating everything to accumulation of means of production, building a state capitalism of their own at the expense of the gains made by workers and peasants in the revolution of 1917. This gave them the means, through large and powerful land forces, to dominate virtually the whole of northern Eurasia, from the borders of Western Europe right through to the Pacific. But with levels of industrial productivity less than half those of the US, they were in no position to sustain themselves in economic competition through free trade.

In 1947 and 1948 they decided to contest the US attempt at global hegemony by blocking its access to the economies under their control— not just the territory of the old Russian Empire, but also the countries of Eastern Europe which they subordinated to their military-industrial goals. The US, for its part, rushed to cement its hegemony over Western Europe through finance to pro-American Christian Democrat and Social Democrat political parties, a Marshall Plan for reviving European industry within parameters favourable to US interests, the creation of the NATO military alliance and setting up US bases in Europe.

The developing conflict cannot be explained by economics as often understood, in terms simply of profit and loss accounting. The armaments bills of both great powers soon exceeded anything their rulers could hope to gain from the increased exploitation of the lesser powers under their control. At no stage in the 1940s or 1950s did total US overseas investment (let alone the much smaller return on that investment) exceed US spending on arms. Even in the period of 'disarmament' prior to the outbreak of the Korean War 'military expenditure totalled something like $15 billion a year. Thus it was not only 25 times as high as the sum of private capital exports, but it was also many times greater than the sum of foreign aid. Marshall aid did not total more than $5 billion in any one year'.[60]

Thirty years later US overseas investment had grown many times over. The total was now about $500 billion ($200 billion of direct investment plus bank loans worth perhaps $300 billion). On top of this there were something like $300 billion of foreign assets controlled by US multinationals.[61] Total expenditure on 'defence' had also risen to around $200 billion—less now than total overseas investment, but still substantially more than the profits that could possibly accrue from that investment.

The picture for the USSR will have been somewhat similar. In the years 1945-1950 it pillaged Eastern Europe, removing plant and equipment wholesale from East Germany and Romania, and forced the region as a whole to accept prices below world market levels for goods going to the USSR proper.[62] But even in that period the economic gains from this must have been substantially less than the escalation of the USSR's arms budget once the Cold War had well and truly begun. And from 1955 onwards, fear of rebellion in Eastern Europe led the Soviet government to relax the direct economic pressure on its states. Their pattern of economic development was still to some extent determined by the strategic demands of the USSR, but direct exploitation seems to have virtually disappeared.

The imperialism which necessitated arms spending was not the imperialism of a single empire in which a few 'finance capitalists' at the centre make huge super-profits by holding billions of people down. This, after all, was a period in which international trade was much less important than it had been before 1914—an index of trade in manufactures as a proportion of world output fell from 1.2 in 1914 to 1.0 in 1930, and then slumped to 0.7 in 1940 and 0.6 in 1950.[63] Rather it was the imperialism of rival empires, in which—as Bukharin had described it in 1916—the combined capitalists of each ruling class had to divert funds from productive investments to military expenditure in order to ensure that they hung on to what they already possessed.

The calculation in both Washington and Moscow was simple. To relax the level of military spending was to risk losing strategic superiority to the rival imperialism, enabling it to seize territory. So the Russians lived in fear of an attempted US 'roll back' of Eastern Europe, which would have broken these economies from the USSR's grasp, leading in turn to the possibility of an unravelling of the ties which bound the other constituent parts of the USSR to its Russian centre (something that did in fact happen eventually with the great economic and political crisis that shook the whole Eastern Bloc in the years 1989 to 1991). In a somewhat similar way, the US ruling class feared the USSR pulling other Western states— in particular West Germany or Japan—into its sphere of influence, enabling it to vastly increase its military-economic potential for challenging US interests everywhere.

As one US spokesman put it at the time of the Korean War:

> *Were either of the two critical areas on the borders of the Communist world to be overrun—Western Europe or Asia—the rest of the free world would be immensely weakened...in economic and military strength to resist further aggression... If Western Europe fell, the Soviet Union would gain control over 300 million people, including the largest pool of skilled manpower in the world. Its steel production would be increased by 55 million tons a year to 94 million, a total almost equal to our own... Its coal production would leap to 950 million tons compared to our 550 million. Electric energy in the area of Soviet domination would be increased from 130 to 350 billion kW hours, or almost up to our 400 billion.*[64]

So the pattern was laid for the next 30 years, of each of the two great powers reaching out to draw as much of the world into its sphere of influence so as to gain a strategic advantage over the other. They fought a bloody war over control of the Korean peninsula, not because of the little wealth it possessed, but because of the strategic implications for the whole of the East Asian and Pacific region. They gave aid and arms to regimes which fell out with their rival—the US to 'Communist' Yugoslavia so as to gain a foothold in the Balkans close to Russia's borders; the USSR to Cuba so as to get a toehold in the Caribbean close to US borders; the USSR armed Somalia to fight an Ethiopia armed by the US, and then, in a quick turn around, the USSR armed Ethiopia and the US Somalia; Egypt was pulled into the Soviet sphere of influence briefly, and China left it to make an ad hoc arrangement with the US.

Even this might not have been enough to explain the sheer level of military expenditure at the height of the Cold War—equivalent to nearly 20 percent of US national output and probably twice that proportion of the substantially lower USSR national output.[65] But arms expenditure had one other great advantage for US capitalism. A massive upsurge in spending by the state on armaments during the Second World War to over 40 percent of national output had had the unintended consequences of providing a market for private capital, pulling it out of the developing recession of 1937 to 1939 and permitting a doubling of total output without lowering the rate of profit.[66] During the Cold War there were similar gains with a lower level of arms spending (see figure 3). Profit rates remained more or less constant through the 1950s, sustaining investment and preventing the economy experiencing the sort of devastating slumps it had known 20 years before. One of the great absurdities of capitalism—that the destruction of value can alleviate the tendency to periodic crises[67]—encouraged the great arms race between the two rival imperialisms of the Cold War years.

The Cold War clash of imperialisms came to an end with the collapse of the Soviet Bloc in the late 1980s. But during its course enormous changes had taken place within the structure of world capitalism as a whole.

The end of the European empires

The Second World War fits neatly with the theory of imperialism as expounded in 1916, especially by Bukharin, but not with the emphasis taken over by Lenin from Hobson on financial capital and investments overseas. So do the 40 or so years of the Cold War, although in a way not recognised by many on the left at the time (and some still today).

Britain, France, Holland and Belgium reacted to the defeat of Germany and Japan by re-establishing their hold over their old colonial possessions in the Far East, North Africa and the Middle East—even if France often relied upon British or US troops to retake colonies for it. There were also attempts to maintain independent imperialist policies, with Britain developing its own nuclear weapons since key sections of its political establishment did not trust the US to defend its interests at all times. Britain maintained its own military presence 'east of Suez', at considerable cost to itself, until the late 1960s. Britain and France together embarked on one last military adventure in defiance of the US with the Suez war of 1956.

But the trend in the post-war decades was away from the colonial policies and conflicts between Western capitalist powers, as theorised by Lenin and Bukharin, which had characterised the previous 70 years. Britain finally abandoned attempts to hang on to the jewel in the colonial crown, the Indian subcontinent, in 1947 after a major mutiny by its Indian sailors, and began in the same year a long retreat from the eastern Mediterranean. Malaysia and the African colonies were to follow in the next two decades. Dutch imperialism tried to hang on to the East Indies, but had conceded defeat by 1950. French resistance to abandonment of empire was stronger—an unsuccessful nine-year war to hold on to Indochina was followed by an equally unsuccessful nine-year attempt to keep Algeria, but by the 1960s it too gave up all of its formal empire apart from a couple of islands in the Caribbean and Pacific.

The US replaced Western European influence in some regions. It took control of South Vietnam when the French withdrew in 1954—until it too was forced to withdraw after the most bitter of wars in the mid-1970s. It became the dominant influence in most of the Middle East and parts of Africa. But, like the European powers, it retreated from formal colonisation, granting independence to the Philippines and keeping direct control only over Puerto Rico.

This retreat from direct colonisation had as a direct corollary the end of the old clashes between the Western powers over the partitioning of the rest of the world. The drive to war between them seemed to have gone once and for all. It was also accompanied by something else unexpected by the Lenin and Bukharin theories of imperialism—once divested of their colonies, each of the Western economies participated in a boom that eventually lasted more than a quarter of a century, saw minimal unemployment, and maintained profit levels without apparent trouble despite regular rises in living standards for their workers. And the advanced countries without any colonies—West Germany, Japan and Italy—had the economies which expanded fastest of all. It almost looked as if Hobson had been right in his claims that colonies were a drain on the economy which would otherwise be able to provide massive reforms at home.

In fact, the driving force behind the boom was precisely the Cold War imperialist rivalry between the US and the USSR, with its massive arms expenditure. Far from there being a 'surplus' of capital in the advanced countries, there was a shortage, and the exports of capital stayed down at the very low levels they had sunk to in the great slump of the 1930s.

As Mike Kidron pointed out in 1962:

Even in Britain…the significance of capital exports has declined tremendously: latterly they have run at about 2 percent of gross national product compared with 8 percent in the period before World War One; they now absorb less than 10 percent of savings compared with some 50 percent before; and returns on foreign investment have been running at slightly over 2 percent of national income compared with 4 percent in the 1880s, 7 percent in 1907 and 10 percent in 1914. Between 1895 and 1913, 61 percent of all new capital issues were on overseas account; by 1938 they were down to 30 percent and more recently accounted for no more than 20 percent of the total.[68]

And foreign investment was decreasingly directed towards the less industrialised parts of the world: 'The concentration of activity is increasingly within the developed world, leaving all but a few developing countries outside the reach of the new dynamism'.[69]

The figures for the Latin America show the decline in the importance of foreign investment in the post-war period:

PERCENTAGE SHARE OF FOREIGN DIRECT INVESTMENT IN DOMESTIC CAPITAL STOCK

Argentina	1913: 34	1940: 16	1950: 3	
Mexico	1910: 49	1940: 32	1950: 26	1970: 9

The last figures can be compared with those of Canada, where the figure was 8 percent in 1950 and 12 percent in 1970.[70]

A shift in the demand for Third World products took place at the same time as the changing in the pattern of investment. At the beginning of the First World War raw materials from agricultural countries were indispensable for industrial production in the West, and colonial control was an important way for industrialised countries to ensure their own supplies and block access to their rivals. But the interruptions to trade during the two world wars forced them to try to find substitutes for such raw materials. So the first half of the 20th century saw the invention of artificial fertilisers, synthetic rubber, rayon, nylon and a vast range of plastics. And during and after the Second World War there was a massive transformation of agriculture in both Europe and North America, with the use of industrial outputs and subsidies to raise food output, so reducing reliance on imports from the rest of the world. In a world now awash with raw material and foodstuffs, withdrawal from colonies in Africa and Asia was no longer the threat it would once have been to the industrialists of the European countries, and companies which had made their fortunes from such things now began to diversify their investments into new lines of business. By the early 1960s the bigger firms in Britain were consciously shifting their focus from the lands of the old empire to the new markets in Europe and North America.

There was, however, one great exception to this picture—oil. Here was the raw material of raw materials, the ingredient for manufacturing the plastics, the synthetic rubber and the artificial fibres, as well as providing for massively expanding energy needs and propelling the ever greater proliferation of motor vehicles, tanks and aircraft. And the supplies of it were increasingly to be found outside Europe and North America. In the early 1950s 'gulf oil' referred to reserves to be found around the Gulf of Mexico, especially in Texas. It was cost of pumping out that oil that determined world prices. By the mid-1970s, as was shown by the temporary interruption of supplies during the Arab-Israeli war of 1973, the gulf that mattered was the Persian Gulf. Saudi Arabia, Iraq, Iran, Kuwait, the petty sheikhdoms around the Arabian peninsula, were the countries that mattered. Control over their policies became increasingly important for the advanced capitalist states. Bribes, threats, weapons sales, the deployment of military 'advisers' and seconded troops were used to achieve this—and so was support for the world's last classic colony, the Israeli settler state with its expulsion of most of the indigenous population and denial of rights to the rest. It was in this region that the wars that mattered for the world system increasingly took place—in 1947-1948, in 1956, in 1967, in 1973, in 1980-1989, in 1982, in 1991, in 2003.

The Third World after colonialism—coming to terms with harsh realities

The dismantling of the European colonial empires was a political fact of immense importance for something like half the world's people who had lived under the thumb of such empires. It raised very important questions for those who had, in one way or another, fought against the hold of those empires. What happened to imperialism—and the fight against it— if empires no longer existed?

The reaction of many social democrats and liberals in the West was to say that imperialism no longer existed. This was, for instance, the conclusion drawn by the most widely known populariser of Marxism in Britain in the 1930s, John Strachey. In his *End of Empire* (1959) he argued that a combination of trade union pressure and government intervention had raised living standards, so that businesses no longer needed colonies to absorb the surplus and prevent overproduction. In effect, he was saying that Hobson's alternative to imperialism, a reflation of the domestic economy, had prevailed and solved the system's problems.

An important section of the left rejected such reasoning. They could see that the former colonial countries were still plagued by poverty and hunger—and that the Western firms that had benefited from empire remained entrenched in them. What is more, the end of the European empires was not the end to the violence inflicted on the peoples of what was now called the 'Third World' or the 'South'. In many places the US state was picking up the baton of violent oppression from the departing Europeans. The French had hardly left Algeria before US troops were inflicting terror on Vietnam, and the US withdrawal from Vietnam was hardly over before it was backing attempts by apartheid South Africa to send troops to tear apart Angola, recently liberated from Portuguese rule.

Rejecting facile talk about an end to imperialism usually meant insisting on the continued relevance of Lenin's 1916 analysis without recognising the changes that had occurred since it was written. Yet there was a real problem. The very strength of Lenin's approach rested on its insistence that the great Western powers were driven to divide and redivide the world between them, leading to war on the one hand and direct colonial rule on the other. This hardly fitted a situation in which the possibility of war between Western states seemed increasingly remote and colonies had gained independence. Instead most of the left quietly redefined imperialism so as to refer simply to the exploitation of the Third World by Western capitalist classes, ignoring the drive towards war between imperialist powers so central to Lenin's theory, and in practice seeing the whole system as a version of the ultra-imperialism forecast by Kautsky. At the same time they simply replaced talk of colonialism with talk of 'neo-colonies' or 'semi-colonies'.

Lenin had written of 'semi-colonies'. For him these were places like China at the time of the First World War, where colonial armies occupied enclaves of territory and used force to impose their will on the national government. They were countries where independence was a sham, concealing continued subordination to political control by forces in partial occupation of the country. There were some places where things did seem like this after the end of direct colonial control in the 1950s and 1960s. In many cases the departing colonial administrations were able to ensure that their place was taken by their own creatures. The new rulers were people who had collaborated with colonial rule in return for class privileges or a small share in its spoils, and there was enormous continuity in the personnel of the state, especially when it came to key positions in the armed forces. So, for instance, when France was finally forced to abandon Algeria, it also granted

'independence' to huge areas of West and Central Africa by handing power
to people who continued, as in the past, to work with French companies,
use the French currency—and invite French troops in periodically to maintain 'order'. It was hardly surprising that in such instances people spoke of
'neo-colonialism'.

But in some of the most important cases independence did mean independence. Governments proceeded not only to take seats in the United
Nations and set up embassies all over the world. They also intervened in
the economy, nationalising colonial companies, implementing land
reforms, embarking on schemes of industrialisation inspired by the
preaching of the Latin American dependency theorists or, often, by
Stalin's Russia. Such things were undertaken with varying degrees of
success or failure in India, Egypt, Syria, Iraq, Algeria, Indonesia, Ghana,
Equatorial Guinea, Angola, Taiwan and South Korea, as well as by the
more radical regimes of China, Cuba and Vietnam.

Over time even some of the 'docile' ex-colonial regimes began to
follow the same path. This was true, for instance, of the Malaysian
regime (run by politicians fostered by the British in order to crush the
anti-colonial insurgency of the late 1940s and early 1950s), of the Shah's
regime in Iran in the 1960s and early 1970s (brought to power in 1954
after a coup fostered by the CIA), and of the Taiwanese regime (established with US support after the victory of the People's Liberation Army
on mainland China in the late 1940s). Even Mobutu, brought to power
with the help of the CIA in Congo-Zaire in 1965, nationalised the mighty
Union Miniere de Haut Katanga mining corporation along with 70
percent of export earnings three years later.

To call regimes like Nasser's Egypt or Nehru's India 'neo-colonial' or
'semi-colonial' was a travesty—as it was with the classic 'developmentalist' regimes of Vargas in Brazil, the PRI in Mexico, Peron and those
who ousted him in the 1950s in Argentina, or for that matter the nationalist regime run by Fianna Fail in Ireland from the early 1930s onwards.
In each case, attempts were made to establish not only independent political entities, but also independent centres of capital accumulation. These
still operated within a world dominated by the much stronger capitalisms
of the advanced countries, but they were by no means mere playthings of
them.

The success of such attempts varied enormously from place to place. A
handful of countries made it into what might be called the 'second division'
of advanced capitalism. This was true of South Korea, Taiwan, Singapore
and Hong Kong—and by the 1990s of coastal China as it experienced
industrial growth rates much higher than anywhere else in the world. In
each of these cases the imposition of dictatorial regimes and the use of
harsh repression to hold down the living standards of the mass of the popu-

lation resulted in 30 percent or more of output being used for accumulation and successful industrialisation. But similar methods in many other places had very different outcomes. In the major Latin American countries nearly half a century of successful if slow accumulation was followed, in the 1980s, by a 'lost decade' of stagnation, debt crises and increased impoverishment of wide sections of the population. Argentina, an industrialised country whose workers once had living standards as high as those in France, began to stagnate from the early 1970s onwards. Sub-Saharan Africa underwent more than 30 years of falling output per head.

Even where 'development' did take place, it was usually accompanied by a combination of dictatorship and appalling conditions for the mass of people. This is why the feeling that nothing had changed with decolonisation was so widespread among sections of the middle class, workers and peasants. Inevitably there was growing disillusionment among the lower middle class and the workers—and sometimes sections of the peasantry—with the nationalist 'developmentalist' state. It became increasingly clear that it could not fulfil the promises it had made to improve the living standards of the mass of the population and improve the life chances of the middle class. This could easily translate into the feeling that it had betrayed the goal it had proclaimed of 'national liberation'. Opposition movements took up its old slogans and directed them against it—even when, as in Argentina in the 1950s or India in the 1960s, the direct links between the state and foreign capital were still minimal. The nationalist ideology of the bourgeoisie and petty bourgeoisie seeking capitalist development became the left nationalist ideology of those who had suffered from the attempts at such development.

One expression of this was the popularity, particularly after the Cuban Revolution of 1959, of new, radical versions of dependency theory which fused the Stalinist and Latin American traditions and hegemonised much of the left worldwide in the 1960s. The writings of Paul Baran (especially *The Political Economy of Growth*) and André Gunder Frank ('The Development of Underdevelopment') dominated most Marxist thinking on the subject (even though Gunder Frank did not see himself as Marxist).[71]

Baran wrote, 'Far from serving as an engine of economic expansion, of technological progress and social change, the capitalist order in these countries has represented a framework for economic stagnation, for archaic technology and for social backwardness',[72] and, 'The establishment of a socialist planned economy is the essential, indeed indispensable, condition for the attainment of economic and social progress in underdeveloped countries'.[73]

Gunder Frank was just as adamant:

> *Short of liberation from this capitalist structure or the dissolution of the world capitalist system as a whole, the capitalist satellite countries, regions, localities and sectors are condemned to underdevelopment…No country which has been tied to the metropolis as a satellite through incorporation in the world capitalist system has achieved the rank of an economically developed country except by finally abandoning the capitalist system.*[74]

'Socialism' for Baran and 'breaking with capitalism' for Gunder Frank meant following the model of Stalinist Russia.[75]

The 'dependentist' argument, in either form, was a weak one. It rested on four unsustainable assumptions.

It assumed that capitalists from the advanced countries who invested in the Third World deliberately chose not to build up industry, even when it would have been profitable to do so, for fear of competing with industrial capital in their home states. So much of Gunder Frank's argument is of the circular form: industrial development did not take place because foreign merchant capital predominated, and this shows industrial development was stopped by foreign capital. This assumption, of course, was completely opposed to Lenin's belief, based on the experience of pre-revolutionary Russia, that foreign capital could go into the building of industry. It also failed to account for the considerable industrial development that had taken place in Argentina and the British dominions before the First World War and in Mexico, Argentina and Brazil from the 1930s onwards.

Its second false assumption was that the Western states at all time have an interest in using their power to prevent any such industrialisation. In practice, they have done so at some points, but not at others. So Britain followed policies which prevented industrialisation of some parts of its empire, but at other points was quite happy to see industrialisation take place (for instance, with the growth of enormous shipbuilding and engineering industries in north east Ireland, or of jute mills in Bengal).

Thirdly, it assumed that the Western powers were able so to manipulate the Latin American governments as to prevent them following independent policies. Yet the reality was much more complex. Any powerful state has a variety of instruments for bending a less powerful state to its will. But it can rarely achieve more than part of what it wants. So, for instance, Britain did try to influence the outcome of the civil wars that plagued Argentina between the final achievement of independence in the 1820s and the early 1860s. But it was never fully successful, and was usually reduced to trying to make sure the outcome was the least worst from its point of view. The civil wars themselves, and the balance of forces determining their outcome, were a result of internal divisions within the Argentinian exploiting classes (rivalries between the great landowners of the interior and the merchants of Buenos Aires), with each looking for foreign allies to back its claims. This was a very different situation to that which prevailed in Europe's direct colonies or in its semi-colonial enclaves in China—although it had some similarities with Britain's self governing 'white dominions'.[76]

Finally, the theory insisted that because the ruling class of one country was 'dependent' upon its trade and investment patterns with bigger capitalist countries, it inevitably lost any ability to forge an independent path of capital accumulation and economic development. But this would rule out any such independence for most of the world's capitalist countries. For a good half century the European economies, for instance, have been to a high degree dependent on what happens in the US economy (hence the old saying, 'When the US gets a cold, Europe gets pneumonia'). The Dutch economy is to a very high degree dependent on what happens in Britain and Germany. But this has not turned the European ruling classes simply into puppets of the US, or the Dutch ruling class into a plaything of British and German interests.

Dependency theory appealed to people because it recognised the reality that much of the world was not automatically pulled out of poverty simply by embracing capitalism. But its remedy, cutting the poorer parts of the world off from the great concentrations of wealth (including that pillaged by imperialism in the past) in the advanced countries, was not an adequate one. These concentrations of wealth meant that the capitalists of the advanced countries could nearly always outcompete their new rivals—and outgun them if necessary. The USSR may have been able to industrialise (at enormous cost to its people) after 1928. Brazil and Argentina, and later Egypt and India, may have been able to build up some basic industries. But by the late 1960s there were limits as to how much further they could proceed using the model of self contained industrialising. Yet this was the model which dependency theory, whether in its old or its new form, propagandised.

Dependency theory reached its high point of popularity in the late 1960s and early 1970s as the last wave of anti-colonial struggles drove the US out of Vietnam, liberated Angola, Mozambique and Guinea-Bissau from the Portuguese, and ended white rule in Zimbabwe. Yet it was precisely at this time that it showed its inadequacy as, one after another, the old liberated states reached an economic impasse. If there were any doubts, the case of Cambodia proved it. To the praise of some dependency theorists, the Pol Pot regime that came to power in the mid-1970s cut off its economic links with the outside world and tried to follow a policy of completely 'independent' development—and the result was a death toll possibly even worse than that caused by US bombing in defence of the country's previous regime.

Mike Kidron had warned in 1971 that 'independent' development was no longer a viable option in Third World countries. He wrote of, 'the end of a terrible illusion, held as fervently by many seeming revolutionaries as by members of the more orthodox schools: that economic development in backward countries is possible without revolution in the developed'.[77] He was not wholly right. The 'illusion' persisted for a good while longer, and a handful of states that had travelled along the path of 'independent development' at enormous cost to their workers and peasants were able to adopt a new strategy of accumulation based upon opening up their economies to foreign capital and trade. But most were damned whichever path they now took.

Part 3: Imperialism and 'globalisation'

Imperialism had changed from Hobson's time to that of the Second World War. It had changed again in the post-war years. In the late 1960s and 1970s a third change took place.

For 20 years the Western powers were united behind US leadership in their opposition to a Soviet Bloc which was joined by China after the victory of the Communist forces there in 1949. There were occasional tensions between them. Britain and France, as we have seen, tried to wage war on Egypt without US backing, and failed. Sections of the British and French establishment were, at first, fearful of a revived German capitalism, but eventually swallowed their doubts with German rearmament in 1954 and the establishment of a limited economic union between the most important Western European continental states, the Coal and Steel Community (later to become the European Common Market and eventually the European Union). Between 1953 and 1956 there was also fear that Stalin's successors would offer to unite their part of Germany, the German Democratic Republic, with West Germany, in return for the united Germany leaving the Western bloc. Lord Ismay, first secretary general of NATO, described its role for the European powers as being 'to keep the Russians out, the Americans in and the Germans down'.

But these tensions seemed marginal in the face of a series of Cold War conflicts—open war in Korea, eyeball to eyeball confrontations over two very small islands off the China coast, Quemoy and Matsu, the Berlin crisis of 1961 and, finally, the Cuban missile crisis of 1962, which was probably the closest the world came to nuclear war.

Things changed slowly after the Cuba crisis. China began to follow a course increasingly divergent to that of Russia and then in open opposition to it, with near war between the two in 1969 and the visit of US President Nixon to Beijing in 1971—at the height of his war against Russia's ally Vietnam. There were divergences, although never as wide or as open, in the Western camp as well. The European powers did not see any gain for themselves in providing military backing for the US war in Vietnam or even diplomatic cover for its hostility to Cuba. And once he had managed to bring the Algerian war to an end, France's President De Gaulle was openly critical of the way the US used the predominance of the dollar in world trade to buy up overseas investments on the cheap. This led some people to speculate about a new round of inter-imperialist conflict, 'Europe versus America'.[78] But the disagreements never seemed to get out of hand. The US did not put much pressure on its allies to do more over Vietnam or Cuba, and, despite De Gaulle, the other European powers tolerated the expansion of its dollar-based funds in Europe. Hostility to the rival imperialism in the East kept the Western imperialisms co-operating with each other when it came to major issues.

The more important shifts were those taking place beneath the surface.

The economic balance between the various Western states underwent a long term change, as Germany and Japan grew rapidly (see figure 2). In 1945 the US had accounted for something over 50 percent of world output; by the 1980s the figure was down to about 25 percent. In 1953 the US accounted for 59 percent of the advanced countries' combined GNP, and by 1977 only 48 percent; in the same period Japan's share rose from 3.6 percent to 13.2 percent, and of West Germany from 6.5 percent to 13.2 percent.[79] In the early 1960s Japan's manufacturing exports were less than a third of the US's; by the late 1970s they were at the same level. And, after a small downturn with the world economic recession of 1974-75, they continued to grow more rapidly than the US's for another decade. The US—and to a lesser extent Britain—were paying the price of sustaining the whole world economy through arms spending. Essentially the US's arms industry kept its economy booming, and so provided a market for German and Japanese exports. Meanwhile, without massive arms bills themselves, Germany and Japan were able invest more in industry and begin to catch up with the US in terms of productivity and competitiveness.

Along with this went a second great shift within the system as a whole. From the late 1960s onwards there were growing financial flows across national boundaries. Foreign currency commitments of West European banks increased eightfold between 1968 and 1974. The flows sped up massively after the quadrupling of world oil prices in 1973-1974. Oil producing states were suddenly in receipt of enormous funds which their rulers mostly deposited in US banks, which then in turn lent them to certain newly industrialising countries (especially Brazil) and Eastern Bloc countries (Poland and Hungary). These were still booming and seemed to offer a safe return on the loans. The booms did not outlast the next world economic recession in 1980-1982, and difficulties in paying interest on the loans brought the countries to the verge of bankruptcy. But the circuits of finance continued their expansion. By September 1985 total lending to the world banking system totalled $2,347 billion,[80] and the Eurobond market increased 70 percent in size in that year alone.

Parallel with the growth in international banking went an explosive expansion of international currency deals which made attempts by governments to control national banking systems seem increasingly futile. As the *Financial Times* noted in the mid-1980s, 'Deregulation and technological advance' was pulling 'the world banking market into a single great pool of capital',[81] and leading to 'visionary phrases' from 'top international bankers' such as 'globalisation of securities markets' and 'serving the customer in a single world marketplace'.[82]

The growth of finance was accompanied by a resurrection of the feature Hobson, Hilferding and Lenin had paid so much attention to—the export of capital. The stock of foreign direct investment (FDI) had amounted to only 4 percent of world gross domestic product in 1950 (as against 9 percent in 1913). In 1999 it reached 15.9 percent.[83] Total world FDI outflows amounted to $37 billion by 1982. By 1990 they had shot up to $235 billion and in 2000 to $1,150 billion. By the last date they were equivalent to around one sixth of total world fixed capital formation.[84] But there was one major departure from the Hobson-Lenin picture. The flows were not from industrial to 'under-developed' countries. They were overwhelmingly to areas where industry already existed.

'The key point to notice is that stock of both inward and outward FDI are concentrated in the developed economies; the overwhelming share of FDI flows is between developed countries'.[85]

There was a rise from 25 to 30 percent in the share of FDI going to 'developing' countries between 1980 and 1990, but 'within the developing countries themselves these stocks are highly concentrated among a handful of countries... If China is excluded the share of inward stock held by the developing world has been more or less stagnant over the last 20 years... Ten developing countries received 80 percent of the total FDI flows to the developing countries'.[86] Europe alone accounted for around half of US direct investment overseas in the mid 1990s, 50 times more than Indonesia and nearly 400 times as much as India, even though India's population is around four times larger than Europe's.[87]

Such flows of investment are an indication of where capitalists think profits are to be made, and they suggest that it is overwhelmingly within the advanced countries, and a handful of 'newly industrialising' countries and regions (of which coastal China is now the most important). This means that, whatever may have been the case a century ago, it makes no sense to see the advanced countries as 'parasitic', living off the former colonial world. Nor does it make sense to see workers in the West gaining from 'super-exploitation' in the Third World. Those who run the system do not miss any opportunity to exploit workers anywhere, however poor they are. But the centres of exploitation, as indicated by the FDI figures, are where industry already exists.

The rise in the figures for FDI reflects very much the rise of the multinational corporations. Multinational firms (eg ITT, Ford, Coca-Cola) had existed in the pre-war period. But they were not generally based upon integrated international research and production. The British subsidiary of a US car firm would in general develop and market its own models independently of what happened in Detroit. It was this that began to change in the 1960s and 1970s. The successful firms began to be those who operated international development, production and marketing strategies. Already by the late 1950s IBM (bolstered by huge contracts for the US military) was able to dominate the new mainframe computer industry worldwide. Boeing (again bolstered by US military contracts) began to drive rival 'national' civil aviation firms into the ground, forcing European firms to pool their resources in the Airbus consortium. Petrochemical production ceased to be confined within individual European countries and came to involve elaborate pipelines carrying materials from plant in one country to plant in others. A new stage of capitalist production, based upon multinational enterprises, had arrived.

Once the process of internationalisation of production was under way, there was no stopping it. By the late 1980s there was hardly an industry in which firms in one country did not have to work out international strategies, based upon buying up, merging with or establishing strategic alliances with firms in other countries. Not all these mergers and alliances survived the ups and downs of the world economy over the next two decades. Some de-merged or divorced, only then to link up with other rivals. But the overall pattern was set. Firms which wanted to survive growing international competition had to embark on buying up affiliates abroad. By 2001 European companies were spending $126 billion buying companies in the US, and US firms $42 billion buying companies in Europe.[88] Some 80 percent of FDI in 1999 was on buying up foreign firms, as opposed to starting up new production facilities (so much for the neo-liberal myth that foreign investment always means increased output and jobs).[89]

The state, capital and 'globalisation'

The internationalisation of finance, markets and production led, in the mid-1990s, to many people making a simple judgement. The state was disappearing as an economic actor. A new multinational world capitalist class was emerging which had no need for this relic of half a century ago. The judgement was wrong. It failed to recognise the continued interconnectedness of the biggest multinationals and the most powerful states.

A big portion of the sales and the bulk of the investments of the major multinationals remain concentrated in their home country (or, for small countries, in that and adjacent countries). A detailed survey showed this ten years ago.

PERCENTAGE OF BUSINESS FOR MULTINATIONALS IN HOME COUNTRY [90]

	Manufacturing sales	Service sales	Manufacturing assets	Service assets
US	64	75	70	74
Japan	75	77	97	92
Germany	48	65	n/a	n/a
France	45	69	55	50
UK	36	61	39	61

The extreme concentration of assets in the home country for Japan and the US was apparent. Of the *Fortune* 100 largest firms, 40 did half or more of their sales in foreign markets, but only 18 maintained the majority of their assets abroad, and only 19 at least half their workforce.[91] The picture was slightly less clear cut in the case of the European multinationals, because many have begun investing in neighbouring European countries, but if the European Union was treated as a 'home region', degrees of concentration comparable to those in the US and Japan were found. British multinationals were an exception, in that over 20 percent of their assets were in the US, a similar figure to that for continental Europe. Both figures were, however, much higher than for assets located in the whole of the rest of the world combined (including the much-hyped Asian 'Tigers'). The internationalisation of the system has proceeded apace over the last decade. But the changes have been quantitative, not qualitative. So in 1998 inward foreign investment was only equivalent to 10.9 percent of private domestic capital formation in the developed countries—leaving local investors responsible for nearly 90 percent. A survey of 498 top Japanese firms shows that just over a quarter of their profits come from overseas—which means they still depend for nearly three quarters on the domestic market.[92]

At the same time, most major multinational firms remain firmly controlled by capitalists from a particular country. Again, the most thorough figures come from ten or a dozen years ago. Of 30 US 'core' firms, only

five had a foreigner on their executive board in 1991, and only 2 percent
of board members of big American companies were foreigners. Only
two of 20 big Japanese companies and four of 15 'core' German firms
had a foreigner on their board.[93] Recent studies suggest that most top
multinational corporations will now have a couple of non-nationals on
their boards. But these remain a small minority. So only ten of the top 35
Swedish companies had any foreign directors in 1999, and these only
accounted for about 10 percent of all directors, while nearly three quarters of the top Dutch companies had no foreign directors, even though 60
percent of the sales of the top companies were outside Holland.
Researchers concluded, 'The national diversity of top management
teams has not progressed at the same rate as the internationalisation of
the companies at large'.[94] Firms with a global reach like ExxonMobil and
Microsoft can operate with no non-US directors.[95] Renault-Nissan refers
to itself as a 'binational group' (French-Japanese), rather than multinational,[96] and the US business media have been screaming that the merger
of Daimler-Benz and Chrysler, instead of living up to promises of a
global corporation, has in fact resulted in a German-run one.

Regardless of the nationality of its directors, what the national state
does can still have an enormous impact on the profitability of a company
operating from its territory. It controls taxation and government expenditure, both of which influence both the general level of economic activity
and the possibilities open to particular firms. Through its influence on the
national bank, it influences the liquidity available to firms and the rates of
interest they have to pay on any borrowing. It is responsible for company
laws and labour laws which affect the balance between different companies, and between them all and their workers. It negotiates trade
agreements which can open up markets in other countries. It ensures that
other states make sure firms get paid for 'intellectual copyright' on new
inventions and discoveries—increasingly important when it comes to
pharmaceuticals, agroindustry and software—at a time when 'piracy' costs
firms an estimated total of $200 billion a year,[97] and continually threatens
to eat into home markets. It has the capacity to intervene to protect firms
against going bust if their profitability calculations go wildly wrong. And
last, but by no means least, it exercises a monopoly of armed force which
can be used against other states.

These functions do not disappear or become less important with the
internationalisation of the system. The last 30 years have seen three
major international crises and the beginning of a fourth. The actions of
states have been very important in determining the survival of certain
major firms and the profitability of many others.

Decisions had to be made on whether to influence currency levels,
whether to raise or lower short term interest rates, whether to enter into

the trade agreements under the auspices of the General Agreement on Tariffs and Trade and then the World Trade Organisation (WTO), how to allocate government contracts, the level of military expenditure. And on top of these there was the question of what should be done with the direct state intervention into the economy though nationalised industries, currency controls, tariffs and so on inherited from the previous period. Even the neo-liberal decision to scrap all these things was still a decision to be made. Multinationals with over 35 percent of their investments (the minimum in our list above) in one 'home' country could not afford to neglect trying to have an impact on any of these choices.

So it was that negotiations between states played a key role in the interrelations between the firms based within them at certain points in the 1980s and 1990s: the 'Plaza Accord' agreement between the US and Japanese governments to shift the value of the yen compared to the dollar so as to make life easier and more profitable for US firms in the mid-1980s;[98] the decision of the European governments to form the European Exchange Rate Mechanism (ERM) and then the euro—and of the British government to escape from the devastating impact of the ERM on the exports of British firms in 1992; the haggling between the European Union and the United States over barriers to trade in agricultural products and over 'intellectual copyright' (essential to raising the profitability of software and pharmaceutical companies); the discussions within the framework of the International Monetary Fund (IMF) over the treatment of indebted countries; agreements over landing rights at international airports; and the sorts of weapons supposedly integrated military pacts were going to use.

How important state decisions could be for very big firms can be seen by looking at the *Fortune* 100 list of the world's biggest firms: 'All formerly or currently leading US computers, semiconductors and electronic makers in 1993 *Fortune* 100 benefited enormously from preferential defence contracts', another 23 were 'directly engaged in the oil industry' and so very dependent upon the ability of their 'home' government to protect their concessions, while at least 20 companies would not have survived at all as independent companies if they had not been saved by their respective governments in the previous decade and a half.[99] On top of this, all the key telecoms firms depended for major contracts and operating licences on governments, and bargaining between governments and international consortia.

The world biggest companies have *both* expanded beyond national boundaries on a scale that now exceeds the internationalisation of the system before the First World War *and* remain dependent to a high degree on their ability to influence 'their' national government. This is because, at the end of the day, they need a state to protect their web of international interests, and the only states that exist are national states.

As Dick Ryan has recently noted with respect to the most internationalised aspect of the system:

> *International finance provides a clear illustration of the centrality of nationality within global accumulation. The combination of satellite and computer technology has provided...all the technical preconditions for the neoclassical 'perfect market' of financial flows to equalise rates of return across financial frontiers and locations, transcending national boundaries. Yet...it is well recognised that finance maintains national characteristics. It does not move systematically so as to equalise savings and investment in each nation... A global financial system comprised of nationally-designated currencies signals that globalisation cannot be devoid of a national dimension. Because nation-states are deemed responsible for the global commensurability of 'their' currency, globalisation, as it actually appears, even in the advanced form of finance, is not about eradicating the national dimension of accumulation. Indeed, globalisation is not even about the national dimension 'hanging on' in a process of slow dissolution. Global accumulation is actually reproducing the national dimension, albeit in ways different to past eras.*[100]

It does not matter how much governments may avow their ideological commitment to 'neo-liberalism' and leaving the economy to the market. They can no more avoid making decisions on things that can have such a dramatic effect on the market than they can jump over their own shadow. And the great multinationals cannot avoid influencing and being influenced by this decision making.

This never consists of the politicians simply responding in a mechanical manner to an agreed policy laid down by capital. For capital is made up of rival firms, each jostling for its own positions—and often of rival bosses within those firms each trying to get one up on the others. There are limits which capitalist governments cannot step outside of without doing immense damage to the economy and to themselves. But within this framework coalitions of capitalist politicians and business interests push divergent policies, each trying to show it can shape out the best policy for the ruling class as a whole. Such coalitions typically combine those motivated by short term profit, those with the big money to dominate the media, the simply corrupt, and those with an ideological vision that gives a section of the capitalist class a sense of historic purpose. The various factions that battle for control of the Republican and Democratic parties in the US are such coalitions. So too are the rival pro-euro and anti-euro groups within the Tory and New Labour wings of the British political establishment. What they are battling over is the use of state power for capitalist ends. It is this which creates the potential for imperialism in the sense of the use of coercion as a form of inter-capitalist competition on an international scale.

The United States: hegemony, force and the second Cold War

The trend towards 'globalisation' began just as the US was suffering its most important military setback of the 20th century—its failure to subdue Vietnam. The US began the war believing it was facing a simple policing operation which its economic and military might would make easy. 'We have 30 Vietnams,' declared Robert Kennedy, shrugging off warnings about potential problems.[101] But as it was forced to double and double again the forces it deployed, it faced not just resistance from those horrified by the war, but also growing opposition to the cost from within the ruling class, with Wall Street beginning to turn against continuation of the war,[102] even though it was no higher than that of the Korean War 15 years before. The change in the world balance of economic forces was hitting at the US's ability to maintain its global hegemony. By the time the war eventually ended there were deep splits in the US political establishment that culminated in Nixon's attempts to spy on the Democratic Party, the Watergate affair and the forced abdication of the president. In the meantime, it had been forced to abandon the Bretton Woods international monetary system which enshrined US financial hegemony, and to begin cutting military spending, which fell in real terms by about 38 percent between the late 1960s and the late 1970s, and as a proportion of GNP by nearly half.[103]

It had lost its old ability to maintain easy dominance over two thirds of the world, just as the internationalisation of the economic system increased the importance of such dominance to its corporations.

For a time it seemed able to cope with a mixture of diplomacy, force and murderous thuggery, doled out by Kissinger, as adviser to Republican administrations, and Brzezinski for the Democrats. The US was able to turn to China as a counterweight to Russia, to use its arms to prevent an Arab victory in the 1973 war with Israel, to pull Egypt fully into the US camp, to help the local ruling class mercilessly crush the left in Chile in 1973 and Argentina in 1976, and to work with European social democracy to contain the Portuguese Revolution of 1974. But then came a triple shock to US hegemony. The revolutionary overthrow of the Iranian monarchy in 1979 suddenly destroyed one bastion of US strategy in the Middle East (the other was, and remains, the Israeli settler state) as Islamic militants seized the US embassy and held its officials hostage. Sandinista insurgents drove out the pro-US dictator of Nicaragua, established an anti-imperialist regime and inspired guerrilla movements in neighbouring El Salvador and

Guatemala. And Russian troops moved into Afghanistan to keep a pro-Russian government in power in face of rising popular resistance.

These shocks preceded another, on the economic front—the second international recession in five years and, with it, increasing success by Japanese companies challenging US capitalism on its home ground. Japanese car firms began to take sales from the US giants Ford and General Motors, while the third US car giant, Chrysler, was only saved from bankruptcy by a government bail-out (and the selling off of its European subsidiaries).

Such events emphasised the degree to which the US hegemony had not been able to recover from the defeat in Vietnam, and pushed its leaders to embrace a new strategy—at first tentatively under Carter and then with relish under Reagan. It represented a return to the 'Cold War imperialism' strategy of confrontation with the USSR—and of using this to try to force the other Western powers to accept the US agenda on other strategic, political and economic fronts.

There were a number of elements to the strategy:

(i) A reversal of the decade-long decline in arms spending, until it was back in real terms (although not as share of GDP) to what it was at the height of the Vietnam War, and the deployment of a new range of weaponry—the cruise and Pershing missile systems. The objective was to face the rulers of the USSR with a choice—accept US strategic superiority in every sphere (including the capacity to stage nuclear 'first strikes' and 'theatre wars'), or increase spending on arms to such a level as to break its own economy. This was the 'Bukharin' model of imperialist competition with a vengeance.

(ii) Providing a very high level of arms, logistic support and aid in recruiting forces (organised via the Saudi government, Pakistan's military intelligence and the Saudi millionaire Osama Bin Laden) for the Afghan resistance, enabling it to bleed and demoralise the Soviet armed forces, much as the Vietnamese liberation movement had demoralised the US armed forces a decade earlier.

(iii) Organising terrorist forces, the Contras, to undermine the Sandinista government in Nicaragua, and providing military funds and training in the 'counter-insurgency' methods practised in Vietnam to right wing pro-government forces fighting guerrilla insurgency in El Salvador and Guatemala.

(iv) Exploiting the increased Cold War tension to pressure the European governments to accept a new generation of US weapons, and to support wider US strategic and economic goals as they had not all been prepared to during the Vietnam War.

(v) Reasserting the dominant US position in the world financial system by taking advantage of financial instability caused by fluctuating oil prices and the threat to the world banking system produced by sudden indebtedness of those 'newly industrialising countries' which had borrowed heavily in the mid-1970s. The US Treasury secretary Brady masterminded the debt negotiations. The outcome protected the US banks, through putting the burden onto the governments of the borrowing countries (even when the borrowing had been private borrowing, as in the Chilean case), and prising them open to US exports and investments through IMF structural adjustment programmes. Meanwhile, the US ruling class made use of the privilege no other ruling class had. The key role the dollar played in world trade enabled it to borrow easily even when its books no longer balanced.[104]

This 'New Cold War' was a new phase of militarised capitalism—of imperialism—drawing together different political and economic elements. It was not simply driven by profits from foreign investment or trade—these never exceeded the cost of the military expenditure, and the markets it opened up were usually marginal from the point of view of US capital as a whole. Nor was it driven simply by the bonus it provided for the arms contractors (as the *Fortune* table above shows, something beneficial to a high proportion of big companies). Rather the different factors formed a synergy, a virtuous circle in which the economy as a whole grew, boosted by arms spending (economists wrote at the time of 'military Keynesianism'), key companies developed new technologies financed by the military, there was an opening up of useful if not central new markets and increased control over economic assets overseas, and the manipulation of the international financial system in US interests.

The synergy enabled the US economy to grow from about 1982 onwards, and to keep growing, with assistance from the Federal Reserve Bank's cut in interest rates, even after the great fall in the world stockmarket in October 1987. As industry began to restructure and real wages fell, profit rates recovered—although to the level of the early 1970s, not to the much higher level of the 1950s. And economic progress was matched by victory on the strategic front. The cost of keeping up with the US cracked the USSR apart. It had to abandon its hold on Eastern Europe in 1989 in the face of popular unrest, and itself disintegrated in 1991. The Cold War had, it seemed, been won, and the economy had been revitalised.

That, at least, was the way the new wave of neo-conservative ideologues holding middling positions in the Reagan administrations (1983-1988) saw it. As far as they were concerned, the US should be much more prepared than hitherto to use force, nuclear force if necessary, to achieve its goals. Nixon's mistake had been not to do this in Vietnam. They were able to play a role in pushing forward the new imperialism, especially in Central America where they were involved in building up the Contras and the death squads in defiance of Congressional decisions, getting funds to do so through arms and drug smuggling. But their time had not yet come.

Despite the belligerence of the Reagan administrations, US troops were rarely directly in battle. They were used against the small Caribbean island of Grenada in 1983, without success in Lebanon in 1986 (when they withdrew after two bomb attacks) and, under Bush, to overthrow the government of a former CIA protege, Noriega, in Panama in 1989. But the memory of Vietnam still ruled out their wider use. The US ruling class relied on others to do the dirty work for it— the local ruling classes in Latin America, the dictator Suharto in Indonesia, the white South Africans and the dictator Mobutu in Africa, Israel and the Saudis in the Middle East. The approach meant backing the dictator Saddam Hussein as a battering ram against Iran, and it emphasised co-operation with France and Germany as well as Britain in Europe, seeing the European Union as a way of stabilising the region under US hegemony.[105]

What is more, there was a tendency to shift away from the aggressive strategy even before the collapse of the Eastern Bloc. The famous 'walk in the woods' between Reagan and the new Russian leader Gorbachev in 1987 led to new proposals for arms limitation, the removal of the missiles from Europe and a new spell of reduction in arms spending, both in real money terms and as a proportion of GDP. The tendency became more pronounced under Bush Sr and the first Clinton administration (1989-1992 and 1993-1996).

The failure of two strategies

This was no accidental U-turn. The approach of the Second Cold War had a central flaw from the point of view of US capitalism. It was directed at breaking apart the USSR and seeing off threats in the Third World. But doing these things did not go very far in dealing with the problems in the most important parts of the world for capitalism—the 'triad' of Europe, Japan and North America, where the great bulk of surplus value was created.

The 'military Keynesianism' produced growth in the US economy, but not as rapidly as in the other capitalist powers that benefited from the US market. By 1992 a committee of the US Congress could fearfully predict Japan overtaking the US economically within a dozen years. Whatever the successes of US foreign policy, the domestic US economy was increasingly dependent upon borrowing abroad to deal with its 'double deficits'—on the government budget and on the balance of payments. George Bush Sr was forced to break his 'Read my lips, no new taxes' electoral pledge in order to try to deal with the budget deficit—and lost the election in 1992 to Bill Clinton, partly as a result. Clinton's more serious tackling of the deficit necessarily involved lowering the proportion of national resources going to arms.

At the same time, the collapse of the Eastern Bloc in 1989 and the disintegration of the USSR in 1991 created new areas of instability and shifts in the global balance of power that did not always automatically benefit US interests. In Europe most commentators at the time believed that West Germany would be the great beneficiary. Already the dominant manufacturing presence on mainland Europe, it was expected to expand economically and achieve greater strategic influence when it absorbed East Germany. Meanwhile, at the other end of Eurasia, China, with an economy enjoying annual economic growth close to 10 percent, stood to gain from the immense weakening of its rival to the north, giving it greater freedom to play a more assertive role internationally.

In these circumstances US governments followed policies based on doing deals with allies and rivals: building coalitions for the 1991 Gulf War against Saddam Hussein—and ensuring he remained in control of Iraq as a bulwark against instability and Iranian influence in the region; putting up no obstacle to German unification and stressing the role of NATO in Western Europe; pushing the Israelis to make token concessions to the Palestinians and then using the CIA to train the Palestinian security forces; working through United Nations auspices to intervene (disastrously, as it turned out) in Somalia; and giving moral and financial backing to the Yeltsin governments in Russia.

The policy was certainly not one of peace. A decline in military spending in real terms did not mean a loss in military strength compared to the rest of the world—by the end of the decade its spending had risen from 30 to 35 percent of the world total. Nor did it mean a loss of interest in new and even deadlier weapons systems: the 'capital intensity' of arms spending continued to rise in the mid-1990s after a brief drop at the turn of the decade. And there were more military interventions in the 1990s than there had been in the 1980s. There was the Gulf War of 1991, the military adventure in Somalia in 1993, the bombing of Serbia in 1995 to enforce a US plan for Bosnia, the pumping of military aid to the Colombian government, and then the full-scale war against Serbia in 1999.

There was also the beginnings of a switch from coalition building with the European powers and Russia to a policy that could be interpreted as, in part, against them. This was especially true after Brzezinski's protege Madeleine Albright took charge of foreign policy in Clinton's second term. The US pushed to expand NATO so as to take in the Eastern Europe states, it made the first moves to draw former Soviet republics like Georgia and Azerbaijan into its orbit, and it played a much more activist role in the former Yugoslavia. These were moves that could be read as undermining Russian influence, but also as trying to pen in the European powers and counter Chinese influence at the other end of Eurasia.

Brzezinski himself said that 'the absorption of three Central European nations into NATO resolved a problem that was considered "impolite" to mention: the "disproportionate power" of Germany'.[106]

Yet the very fact that these moves were made indicated a growing unease about the US's ability to dominate in the post Cold War era as it had for the half-century before. Those who had guided US imperialism through the Vietnam years and after recognised the difficulties, but believed the US had no choice but to accept a certain loss of its old strength. Kissinger was absolutely blunt about this:

> In the post Cold War world the US is the only remaining superpower with the capacity to intervene in every part of the globe. Yet power has become more diffuse and issues to which military force are relevant have diminished... The end of the Cold War has created what some observers have called a 'unipolar' or 'one superpower' world. But the US is actually in no better position to dictate the global agenda unilaterally than it was at the beginning of the Cold War... The United States will face economic competition of a kind it never experienced during the Cold War.[107]

The US, he argued, could only achieve its goals by diplomacy aimed at keeping a 'balance of power' on the Eurasian land masses: 'The domination of a single power of either Europe or Asia...remains a good definition of strategic danger to America... Such a grouping would have the capacity to outstrip America economically and, in the end, militarily... The danger would have to be resisted even were the dominant power apparently benevolent'.[108] Problems would arise because 'in the years ahead Europe will not feel the need for American protection and will pursue its economic self interest much more aggressively'.[109] Finally, he noted, 'China is on the road to superpower status. At a growth rate of 8 percent, which is less than it maintained over the 1980s, China's GNP will approach that of the US's by the end of second decade of the 21st century. Long before that China's shadow will fall over Asia'.[110]

In effect, Kissinger was describing a world of several rival imperialisms, marked by cross-cutting economic and military rivalries, and much more difficult to deal with than the old 'bipolar' model that had characterised the Cold War.

For Brzezinski the problem was similar, although his conclusions not always the same. There was a 'geostrategic triad' made up of the US, Europe and China. Sustaining US influence meant co-operating with the other two powers, but also keeping them in check: 'China is already a major regional player, though not yet strong enough to contest America's global primacy or even its predominance in the Far Eastern region... China is capable of imposing on America unacceptable costs in the event that a local conflict in the Far East engages vital Chinese interests but only peripheral American ones'.[111]

The European Union, he pointed out, now had a population more than a third greater than the US's and a GDP virtually the same. It also had a key strategic position in relation to Russia and China on the Eurasian continent:

> *The transatlantic alliance is America's most important global relationship. It is the springboard for US global involvement, enabling America to play the decisive role of arbiter in Eurasia—the world's central area of power... In the longer run...a truly politically united Europe would entail a basic shift in the distribution of global power, with consequences as far-reaching as those generated by the collapse of the Soviet Empire... The impact of such a Europe on America's own position in the world and the Eurasian power balance would be enormous...inevitably generating severe two-way transatlantic tensions.*[112]

From such a diagnosis, the expansion of NATO and the moves into the Soviet republics made sense by tying to the US a belt of territory and interests occupying the land mass between the European Union, Russia and China. But Brzezinski was careful to stress the positive angles from a US point of view. A united Europe was still far from existing because of the contradictory interests of its constituent states, and their interests tied some of those states quite closely to the US: 'Currently, Europe...is a de facto military protectorate of the US... It is unlikely Europe will be able to close the military gap with the US in the near future'.[113]

The conclusion to be drawn from these analyses was that the US should be more assertive in its diplomacy, laying down the line to the other powers but not breaking off relations with them. This was the approach which the Clinton administration increasingly followed with Madeleine Albright in charge of foreign policy. The policy in former Yugoslavia typified the approach. Germany, newly emboldened to follow an independent foreign policy in the aftermath of reunification, had taken the decisive step that destroyed the old Yugoslav federation by recognising Croatian independence at a time when the US and Britain were still trying to keep it intact. But the European powers then proved completely incapable of stabilising the situation on their own doorstep. Two moves by the US military—the bombing of the Serbs and the Dayton agreement in 1995, and then the war against Serbia in 1999—were needed to bring back some degree of order to the area. As the US administration saw things, it had proved definitively to the European powers that they needed US military force to keep their own house in order.

Yet this was hardly going to make the Europeans bow down to the US in every set of negotiations over trade, investment or intellectual copyright. The US had still not found a way to cash in on its military power in economic terms. There was continued unease among sections of the its ruling class as to where its policies were leading.

As John J Hamre wrote in an introduction to one of Brzezinski's writings:

> *A national consensus about how the US as a 'hyperpower' should navigate the world is as illusive as ever... The lack of a broad consensus has provided a great opportunity for special interest groups to impose their priorities on the policy making process...[with] increasingly segmented analyses of developments across the world... No overarching theory has emerged, no comprehensive strategy has succeeded in attracting political consensus.*[114]

The ground was ready for the neo-conservatives from the first Reagan administration of 15 years before to make a move.[115]

The Project

The group had an overarching theory, and they began to organise to win key sections of the US political, economic and military establishment to it through think-tanks like the Project for the New American Century and the Heritage Foundation, their paper, the *Weekly Standard*, and innumerable speeches and articles by their key ideologues, William Kristol and Richard Perle. Their starting point was the insistence that the policy pursued under the Bush Sr and Clinton administrations was 'in tatters', in 'meltdown', and that the only thing to stop 'a decline in American power' was a return to a 'Reaganite' policy based on large increases in defence spending, the building of a 'missile defence' system, and action to deal with 'threats' from 'dictatorships' in China, Serbia, Iraq, Iran and North Korea.[116] 'Having led the West to victory in the Cold War, America faces an opportunity and a challenge. We are in danger of squandering the opportunity and failing the challenge'.[117] So went a statement signed, among others, by Donald Rumsfeld, Paul Wolfowitz, Elliott Abrams, Jeb Bush, Dick Cheney, Donald Kagan, Zalmay Khalilzad and Dan Quayle. Another statement in 1998 emphasised the strategic need to take action against Iraq in particular, because otherwise 'our friends and allies in the Middle East and Europe will soon be subject to forms of intimidation by an Iraqi government bent on dominating the Middle East and its oil reserves'.[118]

The signatories of these statements took leading positions in the US government when the Supreme Court handed George W Bush victory in the 2000 election. As economic boom turned to recession and panic about 'terrorism' swept the US in the wake of 11 September 2001, they found very little resistance to their agenda within the administration and

Congress. They were able to push through massive increases in military spending, both in terms of real spending and as a share of GDP, to go full speed ahead with the Son of Star Wars programme, and to unleash war against Afghanistan—and all while providing massive tax cuts for the rich. There was even some discussion within the Bush administration of going for Iraq straight after 11 September, but it was decided that it would be tactically better to go for the easy, less costly target first. It would show the scale of US power, climatise public opinion inside the US to the idea of war, and increase US strategic influence in Central Asia.

These actions amounted to a very sharp turn in US policy. There was some continuity with the latter part of the Clinton presidency,[119] but after 11 September quantity turned into quality. Some opponents of the neo-conservatives regard what took place as virtually a coup by a 'cabal' with 'insane' policies. But their bombastic rhetoric and aggressive wars are an attempt by ardent supporters of the US-based section of world capitalism to solve real problems—just as the colonialist fantasies and racist rhetoric of those like Rhodes who spearheaded the carve-up of Africa in the 1890s expressed the needs of their capitalist class.

The new imperialism and the US economy today

The scale of the problems facing the US economy became clear just as the neo-conservatives were installing themselves in the White House. It had recovered from the recession of the early 1990s and grown some 40 percent by the end of the decade, barely affected by the 1997 recession that began in Asia and swept through Russia and Latin America. By 1999 most mainstream economists were talking of a 'new economic paradigm' which would mean an end to boom-bust cycles, contrasting the US position to that of Japan, which was in virtually permanent recession, and Germany, which was growing slowly.

But the boom collapsed suddenly in the months before 11 September and US companies were found to have been exaggerating their profits by up to 50 percent. Central to the problems was a growing dependence on the rest of the world. The deficit on international trade had not gone away. Advances the US had made in certain important industries (particularly computers and software) had not restored the overwhelming competitive lead it had once enjoyed. Capital expenditure per employee and productivity per hour worked was actually behind France and Germany. Productivity per person employed only remained higher because the working year was over 25 percent longer. The US domestic economy relied on an inflow of funds from abroad, which reached around $300 billion annually by 1999. The cumulative total was a massive $2,500 billion.

Foreign funds continued to flow into the US even when the recession finally came in 2001 and the share prices began a long fall to around half their old level. The US seemed a safer venue for investment than elsewhere, despite low profits, during the period of international instability associated with 11 September and the Afghan and Iraq wars.[120] But there was an ever present risk of a sudden reversal of the trend which might throw the US economy into desperate straits. A quarter of a century of growing international movements of finance, investment, trade and production made US capitalism vulnerable to events beyond its border. Its great multinational corporations needed some policy which would enable the might of the US state to exercise control over such events. The new imperialism of the neo-conservative 'cabal' tried to provide it.

There was one important thing going for the policy. US arms expenditure in 2002 of $396 billion was more than that of Europe, Japan and Russia combined. But it was considerably less than the annual inflow of funds from abroad, now around $500 billion. As Martin Wolf of the *Financial Times* has put it, 'The US current account deficit is 50 percent bigger than its defence spending... Indirectly the rest of the world pays for the exercise of US power'.[121]

The biggest single source of funds flowing into the US is Asia, which accounts for about 40 percent of them (half from Japan). Next comes Europe with over a fifth (less than half from the euro zone).[122] Effectively, although they did not notice it, investors in Japan and to a lesser extent Europe were lending the US the money which enabled it to maintain its global military superiority. This superiority was one factor making the US seem a 'safe' haven for investors in East Asia and elsewhere in turbulent times, encouraging their governments to hold very large amounts in dollars (or dollar-denominated bonds), and so providing the wherewithal for US firms and consumers to buy more from the rest of the world. It was a virtuous circle allowing US capitalism to keep coping, for the time being at any rate.

The policies of the neo-conservatives consisted of upping the military dimension in an attempt to make the circle even more beneficial. Increased arms spending and massive cuts for the rich were meant to pull the US out of recession, just as the 'military Keynesianism' of Reagan had two decades ago. And increased military capacity would ensure the rest of the world accepted policies beneficial to US corporations—acceptance of US rules on patents and 'intellectual copyright' which are so important to the software and pharmaceutical companies, the setting of global oil prices to suit US interests, the continued domination by US firms of the international arms trade and the opening up of foreign markets to US goods. The US Space Command document 'Vision for 2020' had, after all, compared the US military effort to the way 'centuries ago nations built navies to protect and enhance their commerce'.[123]

The returns of trade alone would not make increased arms spending rational for the US ruling class as a whole, as opposed to minority sectors of it. The total foreign income of US companies in 1991 was only $281 billion—around $100 billion less than the arms budget. Even if you added in the profits made on the US's $900 billion of exports, the sums did not justify paying out nearly $400 billion on arms, let alone raising that total considerably over the next few years. The figures could make sense, however, if increased arms spending led to recovery from recession, further military handouts to finance technical advance for computer, software or aviation corporations, and to an increased capacity to dictate policies to other ruling classes—and all paid for by even bigger investment flows into the US as it demonstrated its overriding power. The strategy amounted to believing the US could more than compensate for losing its old lead in terms of market competition by using the one thing it has that the other powers do not—military might.

The war against Iraq fitted into this by providing a chance to demonstrate the sheer level of US military power *and* to increase control over the world's number one raw material. As A J Chien noted:

> *The oil interest is...multi-faceted, not amounting simply to maximising oil companies' profits. The larger issue is maximising US control, which has a variety of benefits including non-oil profits and geopolitical advantages... One should not fall into the common misconception that the overriding US concern is to keep oil prices low. Sometimes we want them high. In the early 1970s the Nixon administration favoured higher prices... The reason was the perception that Japan and Europe, more dependent on imported energy than the US, would suffer more from higher prices... Higher crude prices were also supported by the Reagan administration in 1986... The issue isn't price but control. The Saudi dictatorship does what we want, but the Iraqi dictatorship does not. That's the problem.*[124]

Ian S Lustick from the University of Pennsylvania, an analyst and consultant on Middle East policy for previous administrations, put a somewhat similar argument:

> *This cabal of neo-conservative warriors* [is]...*fully committed to an American military enforced new order in the Middle East with pretensions and fantasies of democratisation of the region...domination of the oil wealth, establishment of large, semi-permanent military bases in the heart of the region, and the elimination of all pressures on Israel to withdraw from the West Bank and Gaza... This fantasy, this vision...required...war to overthrow Saddam and to gain control of Iraq, and the oilfields and the geopolitical assets it represents.*

To rebuild Iraq is emblematic...of the overwhelming power...of the United States in the post Cold War world...the irrefutable sign of the possibility and rewards of grand-scale unilateralism.[125]

The war, then, was part of a wider strategy of using US military power to compensate for relative economic decline over many years. The aim was to so reinforce US global hegemony as to make other countries accept US policies when it comes to the IMF, the World Bank, trade negotiations though the WTO—and by accepting those polices, to enable the US to continue to get the rest of the world's ruling classes to pay for deficits caused, in part at least, by its level of arms spending.

But merely to pose the issue like this is also to bring out the degree to which it *was* a gamble.

The logic of relying on increased spending on military power to get hegemony in other spheres is to create situations where military power—and the fact that you have it and others don't—matters. It is a scenario of 'war without end', justified by talk of the fight against 'terror' and 'rogue states'. But that confronts the US with the problem of having to take on any challenge to its hegemony, however much it might be tactically inadvisable to do so, for fear of being seen to display global weakness. Just as the logic of fighting in Afghanistan was to force war upon Iraq, so the logic of military success in Iraq is to threaten Iran, Syria and North Korea today, perhaps Venezuela or Cuba tomorrow, and eventually even China if they do not submit to US demands.

Yet the gamble cannot do away with the central problem—the degree to which dependence on flows of foreign finance into the US creates potentially immense instability. It is not difficult to imagine scenarios in which investors in other countries started withdrawing their funds from the US, creating a vicious circle in which the falling value of the dollar led still others to move their funds to apparently safer havens. As that ardent defender of capitalism, Martin Wolf, has correctly observed, 'In military affairs, the US can be unilateralist. But the world of economics is intrinsically multilateral. Those running the world's sole superpower would do well to remember this potentially painful fact'.[126] In the meantime it is by no means certain that Europe, Japan or China will bow to the US at the IMF or the WTO just because it has conquered Iraq.

The 'cabal' is caught, in just the same ways as those who guided US policy before it, between the need for US capital to control the world beyond its borders and the difficulties of doing so by military means alone.

The rival imperialisms

US policy, whether as propounded by Kissinger and Brzezinski or the Project, has long rested upon recognition of diverging and often conflicting interests between the capitals based in different countries. The more the capitals operate internationally and try to control things beyond their borders, the more important the divergences and conflicts become. It was his failure to see this 90 years ago that led Kautsky to embrace the theory of ultra-imperialism. It is the same failure that marks the writing of those who claim that free trade and neo-liberalism rule out conflict today—and of those who speak of 'empire' in the singular rather than of imperialisms in the plural.

Conflicting interests which can be blurred over during periods of boom suddenly re-emerge in a sharpened form during periods of crisis. When market growth is slow and profits rates are falling worldwide, the attempt of any one nationally-based bloc of multinationals to use the state to protect their interests internationally crashes into the attempts of other blocs to do the same.

The interpenetration of nationally-based capitals has reached a point much more advanced than during the period described by the classic writers on imperialism. The World Investment Report 2000 states that for the world as a whole FDI reached 'a record $1.3 trillion in the year 2000... The global expansion was driven by more than 60,000 transnational corporations with over 800,000 affiliates abroad... The top 30 host countries account for 95 percent of total world flows of FDI and 90 percent of stocks'.[127] In the mid-1990s it was possible for some commentators to point out that major economies were still less internationalised than before 1914. That is no longer so. FDI today is equal to 15.9 percent of world GDP, as against 9 percent in 1913, and exports are 22 percent of GDP as against 8.7 percent.[128]

But the movements of goods and capital from country to country are not evenly distributed across the globe. They mainly go through a relatively small number of distinct channels (see figure 1).

Europe
■ Large movements of capital from Europe to North America, and a smaller movement from the US to Europe.
■ Major movements of capital between European countries, which are more important than movements to the US, except in the case of Britain.
■ Significant European capital stocks in Brazil and other parts of Latin America.
■ Significant flows of Western European capital to Eastern Europe— although only about 2 percent of world capital flows go there.
■ Significant European exports to Latin America—these are slightly

bigger than the US's to the southern Mercosur region, but only about a quarter of the US's to Mexico.

Japan
■ Large movements of finance from Japan to the US, and smaller movements of capital to Europe.
■ Strong movements of capital from Japan to East and South East Asia.
■ Increasing capital flows from Japan to Hong Kong and China.
■ Growing imports from East and South East Asia.

The United States
■ A massive accumulated stock of US capital in Europe (about half of total accumulated US foreign investment).
■ Continued medium-sized flows of capital from the US to Europe.
■ Growing US capital flows to coastal China.
■ A massive trade deficit with China based on growing exports from China to the US.
■ Growing US capital flows to Mexico and Canada, and vice versa.
■ Significant accumulated US capital stock in South America.
■ The importance for the US of exports to Canada and Latin America (especially Mexico), which account for about a quarter of its total.
   To this picture must be added:
■ The dependence of the US on imports for about half of its oil needs. About two thirds of these imports come from Mexico, Canada and Venezuela, a third from the Middle East.
■ The overwhelming dependence of Europe and Japan upon oil from the Middle East.
   These facts show that as well as the tendency to globalisation of finance, there is a tendency towards the concentration of complexes of industrial production in the three advanced regions of the world—the so called 'triad' of North America, Europe and East Asia. The capitals based in each of these tend to have concentrations of interests in certain other regions of the world. This leads to differing—and often conflicting— international strategies by the great powers.

Western Europe: The European Union (EU) is an attempt to turn the interpenetration of its different national capitalisms into full-blooded integration, and to create a single European capitalist class with a proto-state to protect its interests worldwide. It has involved trying to harmonise the divergent interests of the old national capitalist classes, especially France and Germany.
   German capitalism's central concern is with its powerful manufacturing interests, whose spread beyond national borders has mainly been to

other parts of the European mainland. This has led to it reaching out to Eastern Europe as a location for modern industrial plant with relatively cheap, already skilled, labour close to its existing investments and markets. French capitalism has a wider range of concerns. It has a politically important agricultural sector, interests in its former colonies in North and West Africa, oil contracts in the Middle East (Iran and, at least until recently, Iraq), and growing service sector investments in Latin America. While the pattern of German development pushes it towards the east, France is pushed to assert itself in the region running from the Atlantic to the Arabian Sea—and both are regions which the US sees as central to its own geostrategic interests. And success for a French-German axis in imposing greater unity on European capitalism would represent a potential challenge to US domination of the world financial system—for instance, the turning of the euro into an international reserve currency on a par with the dollar.

These contradictory interests find expression elsewhere. Part of the US strategy of cementing its global hegemony is to increase its penetration of Latin America through establishment of the Free Trade Area of the Americas (FTAA or ALCA). But although Latin America is the world's most important single region for US exports, an EU document states of the Mercosur countries (Brazil, Argentina, Paraguay and Uruguay), 'The EU is the first trade and investor partner in the region. EU-Mercosur bilateral trade amounted to €48,498 million. The EU is the first investor with €83 billion in the period 1998-2000. The US is the second trade and investor partner with Mercosur... US-Mercosur bilateral trade in the year 2000 amounted to €44 billion.' Not surprisingly, the document adds, 'The recent establishment of the North American Free Trade Area illustrates the significant risks which the creation of the FTAA in 2005 could entail if not preceded by a free trade agreement between the EU and Mercosur'.[129]

Such clashes of interest explain the diplomatic manoeuvring in the United Nations and elsewhere in the run-up to the Iraq war. The US refusal to make concessions to France was seen by conservative French politicians to carve France out of a region where it saw itself as having 'legitimate interests'. And the marshalling by the US of support from the rulers of Eastern Europe, Italy and Spain as well as Britain was a trampling on areas traditionally under a degree of German influence.

Certain mainstream European politicians are drawing the conclusion expressed by former French prime minister Laurent Fabius: 'Europe was unable to make its voice heard in the US because it was divided and lacked a unified defence force'.[130] Andrew Moravcsik reports in the *Financial Times*, 'For some years politicians have found' the arguments for higher European arms spending convincing: 'The logic is irresistible:

FIGURE 1: FOREIGN DIRECT INVESTMENT STOCKS:
THE TRIAD 2001

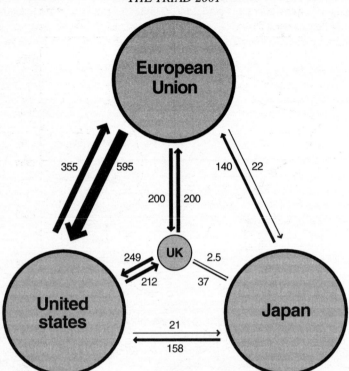

All figures are in billions of dollars and are approximate, depending on changes in the currency exchange rates and the different calculating methods of different governments.

FIGURE 2: CHANGES IN THE RELATIVE SIGNIFICANCE OF
EUROPE, EAST ASIA AND NORTH AMERICA IN THE WORLD
TRADE SYSTEM 1948-1999

	1948	1953	1963	1973	1983	1993	1999
Western Europe	31.0	34.9	41.0	44.8	39.0	43.7	43.0
Eastern Europe*	6.0	8.2	11.0	8.9	9.5	2.9	3.9
East Asia	4.3	5.5	7.2	10.5	15.0	22.2	21.3
North America	27.5	24.6	19.4	17.2	15.4	16.8	17.1

*Eastern Europe includes Central and Eastern Europe, Baltic States, CIS.
Source: based on WTO (2000), Table II.2

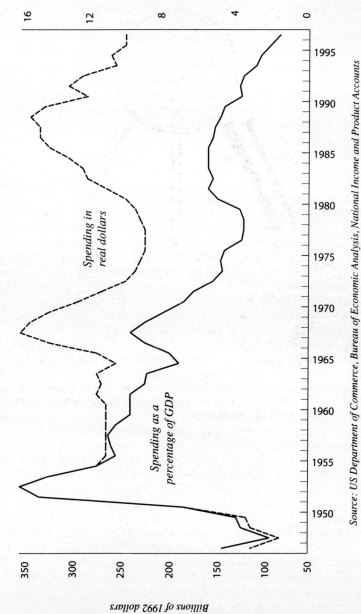

FIGURE 3: UNITED STATES MILITARY SPENDING BEFORE BUSH'S INCREASES

Spending in real dollars

Spending as a percentage of GDP

Percent of GDP

Billions of 1992 dollars

Source: US Department of Commerce, Bureau of Economic Analysis, National Income and Product Accounts

if the US respects only military power, then a European army will surely command respect'.[131]

But attempts to fuse the European capitalisms together in this way have always faced inbuilt obstacles. The companies of each European country value their links to their national states, and fear losing out to rivals from other countries in a transnational European state. What is more, many of them have valued investments inside the US which they do not want to put at risk. As a result, the French-German axis has always been unstable. In the aftermath of the Iraq war German business has been putting pressure on the German government to back off from continued diplomatic confrontation with the US. And, as Moravcsik points out, no government in Europe is likely to accept the cost of creating 'a co-ordinated military force with global capacities to fight a high-technology, low-casualty war'. That would require Europeans to increase military spending, currently at 2 percent of domestic product, to more than the US rate of 4 percent.[132]

There is a capitalist dream of constructing a powerful new European imperialism in place of the competing petty imperialisms. But it will be very difficult to achieve. And, were it achieved, it would be just as barbaric as US imperialism (you only have to look at, say, French interventions in Africa to see why). This is why it is mistaken for people like George Monbiot to suggest the left should back the euro against the dollar.[133]

Japan: For more than half a century its rulers have been content to operate in the US's shadow, allowing the US to occupy one of their islands, Okinawa, as a base, and paying much of the cost of the US's 1991 war against Iraq. The worry Japan has caused the US has been economic, not military. The worries were much reduced in the course of the 1990s. The Japanese economy has stagnated while the US economy has grown, and the industrial restructuring (encouraged by the Pentagon) means US firms again lead in the world computing industry. Japan gave wholehearted diplomatic support to this year's war against Iraq. But the potential for tension remains. Japanese industry has continued to invest heavily through its long recession and could be placed to mount a new economic challenge to the US in the future. And there are sections of the Japanese political establishment who believe it needs to develop its military power to play an independent role internationally—especially in East Asia, where it has important investments and where it could face serious problems if faced with military crises over the Koreas or over China and Taiwan.

Russia: It is an imperialism that has been almost completely on the defensive for more than a dozen years. When they ran the country as heads of the old Communist Party, its rulers regarded themselves as on a par with the US in terms of global influence, and competed with it strategically in areas like South Asia, the Middle East, the Horn of Africa and West Africa. Today it is very much the same class which runs the giant privatised corporations and, through the former KGB secret policeman Putin, the state. And so they too are resentful as they see the US invade a semi-ally, Iraq, and carve out bases (and oil concessions) for itself in Central Asia, in what was once part of their empire.

But they have been cut down in size economically twice—first by losing half of the USSR with the breakaway of the non-Russian republics, and then by the economic crisis which reduced the economic output of what remained by half. An economy that used to be between 30 and 50 percent of the size of the US's is now at most 10 per cent of the size.

They still possess considerable military power. But most of their equipment seems to be at least a technical generation older, and so would not fare very well in conventional battlefield conflicts. They can sell arms to weak countries which want to fight other weak countries, but dare not use it to directly confront those armed with modern US weaponry. And they themselves can only threaten the US with the ultimate suicide weapon, the nuclear warheads of their ageing missile system.

China: The country's coastal provinces have been by far the most successful section of the global system over the last decade and a half, growing somewhere close to 10 percent a year.

But economic successes have also bred important tensions. Hundreds of millions of peasants are witnessing the economic growth without gaining anything from it, as they flood into the cities each year looking for work that is not available. While the coastal areas linked into the world market industrialise at great speed, restructuring leads to massive job losses in the old heavy industrial sectors (which provide important inputs for the new industries). And the unevenness between different regions grows ever greater. Those running the regime fear a recurrence of the Tiananmen Square events of 1989, when protests by students linked up with discontent among workers to produce near-rebellion in most Chinese cities. They also fear fragmentation of the country as those ruling in the regions tied most closely into the world market ignore the demands on resources of the impoverished inland provinces—in some cases provinces inhabited by ethnic and religious minorities who have never fully accepted Chinese rule. Against such centrifugal tendencies, the regime has one card to play—Chinese nationalism. But this leads to tensions with the US over the island of Taiwan, seen by Chinese nationalists as part of their national heritage and by the US neo-conservatives as an integral part of the US sphere of influence.

For the Chinese rulers to concede to the attitude of the US right would, as far as they are concerned, be to concede that they are going to give up part of the historic Chinese Empire. And if Taiwan in the east, why not the extensive non-Han provinces in the north and west? Would it not be a sign to the US right that China could be stripped of its empire and be reduced to a minor power, just as happened to Russia?

A recent *Financial Times* article states:

> *Many analysts argue that it is only a matter of time before Chinese economic power is translated into military muscle... East Asia is a likely theatre for a major war, they argue. A recent report from a US Congressional committee concluded, 'The combination of Chinese leaders' perceptions of America as an adversarial hegemon and the lack of solid bilateral institutions for crisis management response is potentially explosive. In the worst case, this could lead to military conflict.' Hisaiko Okazaki, a conservative Japanese foreign policy commentator and former ambassador, fears that China's growing strength will eventually lead it to take control of Taiwan, thus threatening Japan's strategic supply routes. About 80 percent of Japan's oil supplies come from the Middle East; most of that passes through the Taiwan Strait.*[134]

For some at least of the neo-conservatives in the White House, the Son of Star Wars strategy is directed to cutting China down to size. Paul Rogers of Bradford University has explained their logic:

> *Many on the Republican right think the only threats to US dominance will come from China if it develops into an economic giant. One way to curb its growth is to force it to commit more money to defence, and the National Missile Defence system is one way of doing this. That may stimulate a dangerous nuclear arms race but, after all, the Soviet giant was successfully 'spent into an early grave', and perhaps the same strategy can be applied to China.*[135]

Britain: New Labour prime minister Tony Blair is commonly referred to as George Bush's 'poodle'. This sums up the subordinate position Britain plays in relation to US imperialism. But it also underestimates the degree to which British capitalism has its own imperialist interests. Its investments around the world are second only to those of the US, it is the base of some the bigger multinationals, and it still possesses nuclear weapons. Its problem is that it discovered nearly half a century ago with the Suez adventure that its state is not able to play an independent world role to match the international spread of its investments. Since then Tory and right wing Labour leaders alike have seen the only way to protect its interests as by a 'special relationship' with the US. They could not have won the Falklands/Malvinas War without US assistance, and they have turned to US presidents in the attempt to clear up the mess created by their past actions in Northern Ireland.

The Blair policy during the Iraq war was the logical follow-up to these things. But Blair is finding things are not quite so easy. The decline in the economic importance of the empire in the 1950s and 1960s led sections of British industry to turn increasingly to Europe for markets and investment. And so today British capitalism is pulled in two directions—towards the old alliance with the US and towards those who dream of a new European superstate. Blair would like to reconcile the two pressures by acting as an advocate for the US-oriented sections of British business within Europe. But the recriminations between France and Germany on the one hand and the US on the other over the war are making life difficult for him.

The interaction between the great powers is not the peaceful concert of nations dreamt of by certain apostles of neo-liberalism and free trade, and interpreted as a single entity—'empire'—by Hardt and Negri. There are a set of contradictory interests, with military force a weapon of last resort for dealing with them. The US attacks on Afghanistan and Iraq have shown us that force in action. But there is still a difference with the first four decades of the 20th century. These culminated in wars which ravaged their heartlands. The tensions since 1945 have led to massive accumulations of arms that could potentially be unleashed against the heartlands. But hot wars have been fought outside them, usually in the Third World.

One reason for this has been the 'deterrent' effect, the fear that waging war on a nuclear power will lead to destruction of the whole domestic economy as well as most of its people. Even today, the rulers of Russia, China, India, Pakistan and North Korea—and for that matter Britain and France—see possession of nuclear weapons as the ultimate defence against enemies.

Another has been the very interpenetration of the advanced capitalist economies that puts pressure on states to exercise power outside their own boundaries. Few capitalists want their national state to destroy huge chunks of their property in other states—and most of that property will be in other advanced capitalist countries. This does not rule out war completely. The capitalist economy was highly internationalised in 1914, but this did not prevent all-out war. Again, in 1941, the presence of Ford factories and Coca-Cola outlets in Germany did not stop a US declaration of war after Pearl Harbour. But it does provide them with an incentive to avoid such conflicts if they can—and to settle their differences in less industrialised parts of the world. Hence the years since 1945 have been marked by war after war, but away from Western Europe, North America and Japan. And often the wars have been 'proxy wars' involving local regimes to a greater or lesser extent beholden to, but not completely dependent on, particular great powers.

This has been especially true in Africa. During the last decade and a half of the Cold War the US and the USSR backed rival sides in wars and civil wars as part of their attempts to gain a strategic advantage over each other. Similarly, in South Asia, India was loosely aligned with the USSR and Pakistan more tightly tied to the US (and allied with China). More recently the US and France vied for influence in Central Africa in the early and mid-1990s. They backed rival sides in the war cum civil war that broke out in the border regions of Tanzania, Rwanda, Burundi and Congo-Zaire. They helped set in motion a catastrophe, resulting overall in 3 or 4 million dead. In the same years, the different big powers each developed different approaches for trying to gain advantage from the collapse of Yugoslavia, giving open or tacit support to the different armies that were engaged in mutual ethnic cleansing. In such situations, freelance armies emerged whose commanders emulated on a small scale the great imperial powers by waging war in order to enrich themselves, and enriching themselves in order further to wage war. Imperialism meant encouragement for local rulers to engage in the bloodiest of wars and civil wars—and then, occasionally, the sending in of Western troops to enforce 'peacekeeping' when the disorder reached such a scale as to threaten to damage Western interests. Contradictions which arise from the inter-imperialist antagonisms of the advanced capitalist states in this way make the worst impact in the poorer parts of the world.

War, exploitation and the Third World

If the conflicts between the great capitalist powers find expression in horrific death tolls in wars waged in the Third World, here too the dire economic consequences of their policies for the mass of people are most marked.

Governments throughout the Third World had abandoned attempts at 'independent' economic development from the mid-1970s onwards. Former liberation fighters, supposed 'Communists' and right wing nationalists alike opened up their economies to foreign capital and embraced the 'Washington consensus' of neo-liberalism. This was not just a matter of pressure by the advanced capitalist states, blackmail by the IMF or conspiracies by the multinationals (though much blackmail and some conspiring did take place). The real problem was that the resources available for capital accumulation within the boundaries of any one state, however much protected from outside intrusion, were limited.

Those who had tried to accumulate at home now set out to advance their technology and find wider markets by deals with the world's great multinationals, and to get funds for further development by massive borrowing from the Western banks. As far as they were concerned, they were not surrendering to foreign capital but using it as a lever to raise themselves up. Political parties which had preached the unity of all classes in order to achieve independent economic development now became ardent proponents of collaboration with the multinationals and the world banking system—Fianna Fail in Ireland, the Peronists in Argentina, APRA in Peru, Congress in India, the Communist parties in China and Vietnam.

Collaboration enabled a few sections of local capital to join the multinational league themselves. It enabled others to liquidate their local holdings, and to use the proceeds to invest in more profitable undertakings abroad, making themselves shareholders and bondholders in the advanced economies.

Argentina, Brazil and Mexico were typical. Their industrial bases had been established in the 1940s, 1950s and 1960s by the state intervening to direct investment in industry, often into state-owned companies. But by the 1970s it became clear to the more farsighted industrialists—whether in the state or private sectors—that they could not get the resources and the access to the most modern technologies needed to keep up with worldwide productivity levels unless they found ways of breaking out of the confines of the national economy. They began increasingly to turn to foreign multinationals for licensing agreements, joint production projects and funds—and they began themselves to operate as multinationals in other countries. So the Argentinian steel maker TechNet took control of the Mexican steel tube maker Tamsa in 1993, acquired the Italian steel tube maker Dalmikne in 1996, and then went on to expand into Brazil, Venezuela, Japan and Canada, adopting the name Tenaris. It boasts, 'With an annual production capacity of over 3 million tons of seamless pipes and 850,000 tons of welded pipes, the Tenaris Group is the world leader in the seamless pipe market'.[136] There is a similar pattern with some Mexican companies. In the late 1980s Alfa, the largest industrial group in Mexico, with 109 subsidiaries spanning automotive components, food, petrochemicals and steel, embarked on a growing number of joint operations with foreign firms. Its director of finance said, 'Three quarters of our non-steel business involves joint ventures. We have the culture of joint ventures.' The glass maker Vitro, which had bought two American companies, became 'the world's leading glass container manufacturer, with its market almost equally split between the US and Mexico'.[137] The logical outcome of this in Mexico was for its ruling class to forget its old nationalism, to join the North American Free Trade Area and increasingly operate as a subordinate component of US capitalism.

Occasionally the collaboration produced positive results for wider sections of local capital, provided some job opportunities for the aspirant middle classes (Ireland, South Korea, Singapore, Taiwan, coastal China), and even created conditions under which workers could boost their living standards through industrial action. Usually, however, it created increased indebtedness to foreign banks which the national states had to cope with. In such cases, a narrow stratum of people gained a taste of the fleshpots of multinational capital while the conditions of the mass of people deteriorated, or at best remained unchanged. A yuppie class lived in protected enclaves as if it were in the wealthiest parts of the industrialised world (and often went a step further and lived part of the year there), while much of the population festered in ever proliferating slums and shantytowns.

The results can be seen today in Latin America, where national income per head fell in the 1980s, in the Middle East, where it is lower now than 20 years ago, and above all in sub-Saharan Africa, where absolute poverty has become endemic as the share of world trade has fallen from 3 percent half a century ago to a mere 1 percent today.

Those who run the state face immense problems even when the developmentalist strategy is successful in its own capitalist or state capitalist terms. Its success depends upon a high level of domestic accumulation—and the other side of that, a high level of exploitation that can only be achieved by holding down workers' and peasants' living standards. But even when it succeeds in getting high levels of accumulation (which is the exception rather than the rule), it remains weak in its bargaining with the multinationals. As multinationals take over local firms, their proportion of local capital investment can rise to 40 or even 50 percent of the total, increasing their leverage over local decision making. But states in the poorer parts of the world do not have anything like the same leverage over multinationals, since the small size of their domestic economies mean they probably account for no more than 1 or 2 percent of the multinationals' worldwide investments and sales. As Burke and Epstein have put it, 'Even though foreign investment as a whole is of enormous importance to multinational corporations, it is generally the case that any particular investment in a developing country, with one or two exceptions, is relatively unimportant to them. As result, the bargaining power of political jurisdictions relative to multinational corporations is often very low'.[138] A huge gap begins to open up between what those who run the state have promised the mass of people and what they can deliver. High levels of repression and corruption become the norm rather than the exception. When the developmentalist strategy runs into problems, something else accompanies the repression—the hollowing out of the mass organisations that used to tie sections of the middle class to the state and, via them, some of the working class and peasantry. The oppressive state becomes a weak state and looks to foreign backing to reinforce its hold.

This happens as profitability problems in the advanced countries drive them to look for any opportunity, however limited, to grab surplus value from elsewhere. There is not much to be got from the poorest of the poor anywhere in the world, but what there is they are determined to get. Imperialism means at the top level that the rival capitalist powers argue vehemently with each other on how to satisfy their different interests. At a lower level, it means constraining the local ruling classes of the Third World to act as collectors of debt repayments for the Western banks, royalty payments for the multinationals and profits for Western investors as well as for their own domestic capitalists. Debt servicing alone transfers $300 billion a year from the 'developing countries' to the wealthy in the advanced world.[139] A website dedicated to defending US overseas investment boasts:

> *Most new overseas investments are paid for by profits made overseas. Foreign direct investment by US companies was only $86 billion in 1996… If you subtract out the reinvested earnings of foreign operations, the result was only $22 billion… US companies' overseas operations also generate income that returns to the US… In 1995, this flow of income—defined as direct investment income, royalty and licence fees, and charges and services—back into the US amounted to $117 billion.*[140]

There can be no end to the squeezing. The share of foreign investors in the total amount traded on the Brazilian stock exchange rose from 6.5 percent in 1991 to 29.4 percent in 1995,[141] and the share of new Mexican government debt held by non-residents grew from 8 percent at the end of 1990 to 55 percent at the end of 1993.[142] French and Spanish capital has been highly active in Latin America in this respect. The two big Spanish banks, the Bank of Bilbao and Vizcaya and the Bank of Santander, have bought up a very large proportion of the banking systems of many Latin American countries: 'At present, the biggest Spanish institutions own almost one third of the assets of the 20 biggest foreign banks, which means that they alone exceed the share of the United States banks, which have historically been the leader in this sector in the region'.[143]

The base in banking has been used to branch out into other types of business, 'investment banking, insurance and in particular participation in pension fund management', and to acquire 'minority shares in some non-financial enterprises, basically in sectors where other Spanish investors are very active (telecommunications and energy)'.[144] 'Aggressive strategies adopted by Spanish banks, and also by the Hong Kong and Shanghai Banking Corporation, forced the foreign banks which had already been established in the region for a long time to take defensive measures… Bankers Trust in Argentina and Lloyds Bank, Chase Manhattan and ABN-Anro in Brazil decided to buy local banks or shares in their equity'.[145] The Spanish expansion has been paralleled by the strategy of French firms like Suez and Vivendi of buying up public utilities.

This trend towards taking over the provision of services as a way of guaranteeing a fixed return on capital is, as François Chesnais has pointed out, a growing trend worldwide. The share of services in foreign investment which 'represented only a quarter of the world stock of direct foreign investment in the 1960s amounted to about half by the end of the 1980s and made up 55 to 60 percent of new flows'.[146] Hence the attempts through the WTO to impose TRIPS and GATS measures (relating to payment for patents and to the opening up of public services to the multinationals).

The economies of the Third World are too small a part of the world system for these new forms of financial capitalism to play the same role in solving the problems of the capitalists in the advanced countries that the old forms did in Hobson's time. Argentina's economy, for instance, is no larger than the US state of Ohio's, and even the biggest economy in Latin America, Brazil's, is 20 percent smaller than California.[147] But such squeezing can force people to revolt. The governments of Bolivia and Peru have been shaken by revolts against the selling off of water and electricity supply. Bitterness against the foreign-owned banks and public utilities played a part in the near uprising that overthrew the De La Rua government in Argentina in December 2001. And the resistance can hurt individual companies. The Spanish banks and the French multinational utility companies Suez and Vivendi are now licking their wounds.

The politics of anti-imperialism today

The suffering of the Third World and the revolts against that suffering have been very important in breeding the new wave of anti-capitalism that has been sweeping the world since Seattle. This in turn provided an important part of the impetus for the huge anti-war and anti-imperialist demonstrations at the time of the Iraq war. There is deepening consciousness of those involved in fighting capitalism in the West that they have to solidarise with those resisting oppression in the poorest parts of the world. This is immensely important in helping to undercut the racism and nationalism that has in the past so often bound workers in the advanced countries to their rulers.

At the same time, in the Third World and newly industrialising countries, the nationalism which was the ideology of the developmentalist section of local capital now becomes increasingly double edged. Those suffering from exploitation, repression and political corruption begin to turn it against the most hated local ruling class figures. They are seen as betraying the nationalist agenda, their attacks on the conditions of the mass of the population as a surrender to imperialist pressures. People who were led to believe the state represented the whole nation, rich and poor alike, in the past, now come to see its ignoring of the interests of the mass of people as proving it is a foreign body, a 'new colonial' or 'semi-colonial' state imposed on them from outside. Left nationalism emerges as a current that holds the present state has to be reformed—and can be reformed—so as to remove the foreign influences and re-establish it as a repository of the common, national, interest.

Left nationalism often encourages people to begin to fight against sections of the local ruling class. But its belief that there is some common 'national' interest binding exploiters and exploited together also opens it up to manipulation by the same local capitalist politicians who are working hand in hand with the great capitalist powers. They try to blame policies which suit their interests—like privatisation of utilities or repayment of debt—simply on the pressure of big brother outside. Unfortunately they can often expect some representatives of the popular opposition to such policies to go along with this. So it is common in the Middle East to blame the toleration of the local capitalist classes for Israeli policies in Palestine purely on US pressure (or on 'non-Islamic' behaviour), or in Latin America to see the coups in Chile in 1973 and Argentina in 1976 (or, for that matter, the attempted coup in Venezuela in 2002) as a result just of US plots against 'national independence' rather than as driven by the determination of the local ruling class to crush any challenge to its position, knowing that the US ruling class would back it. Yet almost all the of the wars of the US against insurgent movements since Vietnam have been *proxy* wars, in which it has been able to rely on local ruling classes to wage on their own behalf as well as on its. This was true in Central America for much of the 1980s, when it trained and armed the forces of the right wing governments in Guatemala, El Salvador and Honduras, and the Contras in Nicaragua, with the deployment of only a handful of its own troops as 'advisers' to them. It has more recently been the case with its massive military aid to the governments of Colombia and its encouragement of the coup attempt in Venezuela.[148]

Talk of the state as 'semi-colonial' or 'neo-colonial' reinforces such a misperception. Imperialism is an enemy anywhere. But most of the time the immediate agent of exploitation and oppression is the local ruling class and the national state. These collaborate with one or other of the dominant imperialisms and impose the horrors of the world system on the local population. But they do so in the interests of the local ruling class as well as its imperial ally, not because the local rich have temporarily forgotten some 'national interest' they share with those they exploit.

The failure to see this means that left nationalism, as well as providing a certain focus for the bitterness of the mass of workers, peasants and the lower middle classes, also tends to direct this bitterness towards reformist solutions. At the domestic level, this means fighting for more nationalist as against less nationalist solutions within the framework of the existing capitalist state. A current example of this arises in the struggle against the Free Trade Area of the Americas. Instead of seeking to give an anti-capitalist impetus to this, the non-revolutionary left in Latin America is counterposing Mercosur as some sort of alternative to it. But Mercosur is an attempt by sections of Brazilian big business to hegemonise the other economies of the region and strengthen investment and trade links with the European Union, and does not rule out negotiations over terms of access to the Free Trade Area of the Americas.

At the international level left nationalism means focusing upon issues like the terms of trade or the preference for one trading bloc over another, as if simply improving the terms on which national capitalists sell their commodities on the world market will solve the problems of the mass of people they exploit and oppress. This goes hand in hand with the view that the population of the advanced world as a whole exploit the population of the Third World as a whole, either through 'unequal exchange' or through 'super-profits' made from foreign investment in the Third World. In doing so, it deflects attention from the central dynamics of the world system, which depend to a very large extent on what happens in the most important locations of accumulation, foreign investment and trade—the established industrialised countries, a small number of the newly industrialising countries and, to an increasing extent, the Chinese coastal region. And it undermines the development of real international solidarity.

When Lenin wrote, he called for the workers' movement in the West to see anti-imperialist movements in the colonial world as its ally, but argued strongly against revolutionary socialists in the colonies giving a 'communist colouring' to the 'bourgeois-democratic liberation trends in the backward countries'.[149] The argument needs to be repeated and reinforced today. 'Left nationalist' ideas in the 'developing' and 'newly industrialising' countries can spur people to confront local ruling classes that are tied to imperialism and give rise to near-revolutionary upsurges. But they also, inevitably, misdirect those involved in those upsurges in a reformist direction. This does not matter much for those of us who are active in the West building international activity against imperialism and war. We are on the side of Third World movements against imperialism, however confused their ideas may be. But it is of fundamental importance for Third World revolutionaries. If it was necessary to be critical of such ideas in Lenin's day, when real colonial oppression was directed against sections of the bourgeoisie and petty bourgeoisie in vast areas of the world, it is a hundred times more important today, when the bourgeoisie proper is a fully fledged partner, even if a junior one, of the most powerful sections of world capitalism. It is necessary to be part of the upsurges, but to build independently within them.

The dilemma of US imperialism

US imperialism looked immensely strong in the aftermath of the Iraq war. But none of its central problems have been solved.

Its victory will frighten other governments in the Third World to jump to its orders. It will be that much easier for the IMF to impose its will on countries whose rulers might otherwise be tempted to cave in to opposition from their own people. That is why it was completely wrong for Bernard Cassen of ATTAC France to counterpose opposition to war to opposition to the measures that harm the world's poor.

But the increased exploitation and impoverishment of much of the Third World will not overcome the pressures on profitability and the competitiveness of US capitalism. The fundamental fact that permitted decolonisation without economic disaster for the advanced capitalisms half a century ago remains unchanged. Most investment from advanced capitalist countries is directed to other advanced capitalist countries and the small minority of newly industrialised countries for the simple reason that that is where most profit is to be obtained. Most of the Third World, including nearly all of Africa and much of Latin America outside Brazil and Mexico, is of diminishing economic importance for the dynamic of the system as a whole. Profits and interest payments from such regions are the lettering on the icing on the cake for world capital, not even a slice of the cake itself.

Oil is *the* strategic commodity of the 21st century, and the US has shown by two full-scale wars in a dozen years how keen it is to be in control of it. As I have argued earlier, what matters is not primarily the profitability of its oil companies—giants like Microsoft, Boeing or General Motors are not keen to take the risks inherent in war just for the sake of Exxon. The real concern is controlling the price and availability of oil to provide a stable and beneficial framework, inside the US as well as outside, for profit making and accumulation by US capitalism as a whole. It is also to provide enhanced power when it comes to bargaining with the other advanced capitalist states.

But this cannot resolve the fundamental issue—long term downward pressure on profit rates which had been exacerbated by vast unprofitable investments during the speculative boom at the end of the 1990s.[150] Control of Iraqi oil may be able to help prop up the present precarious domination the US exercises over the world financial system (although, as I write, the dollar is falling) and, with that, allow the US to continue consuming more than it produces. But it cannot add decisively to the proportion of worldwide surplus value controlled by US capitalists. Experts believe it may take up to five years before Iraqi oil comes to flow in sufficient quantities to pay the costs of rebuilding what US bombs and tanks have knocked down. And even then there will be difficult choices to be made. Increasing output on such a scale as to lower the international price of oil substantially, so helping the US capitalist class as a whole may lead to a collapse of the oil revenues needed to pay the construction companies and keep up oil company profits.

Apologists for the war tried to use such calculations to claim the war was not about oil.[151] Their argument was wrong, because oil is an important weapon in the struggle for global hegemony. But some of their calculations were right. Control of oil will not in itself make the tens of billions of dollars spent on the war into a profitable investment for US capitalism.[152] It will certainly not cover the costs of a long term colonial occupation of Iraq—especially if instability as a result of the occupation leads to social upheavals and military intervention elsewhere in the region. Yet the very nature of the US victory in Iraq is likely to make long term military occupation inevitable.

The determination of the Bush gang to hammer home the US's global military strategy by going to war without allies (apart from Britain) ensured they blitzkrieged their way to Baghdad without establishing the prerequisites for the quick establishment of a stable new pro-US regime. In the aftermath they are faced with the choice between staying for a very long period of time or putting in Iraqi clients who may not be able to keep control of the country as a whole—and who may eventually be tempted to use the oil revenues for their own ends (as the Ba'athists did after the US helped bring them to power in 1963 and 1968).

This choice was causing splits within the Bush administration's 'unilateralist' war camp the very day after the conquest of Baghdad. On the one side stood 'liberal imperialists', with their dream of overturning the whole Middle East and running it through supposedly stable capitalist democracies which could provide long term legitimacy for the protection of imperial interests—an Arab version of the settlement imposed in Central America at the end of the 1980s. On the other were 'realist imperialists', eager like Kissinger before them to do deals with any dictator in order to exercise control at minimal cost to the US itself and without US troops getting involved in long term commitments. And in the background is the possibility of a deal with Europe, Russia and China for 'multilateral' or 'United Nations' efforts to bring stability. But such a deal would eliminate direct US control and cancel out some of the gains made by it in the war.

The probability is that the US will fall between all three stalls. It will be compelled to stay in occupation for a long time, logging up the budgetary costs at home and stoking the fires of resistance throughout the Middle East. It will play with local politicians who, lacking any real base, would only be able to stabilise their rule by resorting to the dictatorial methods carried to such heights by Saddam during and after his period as a US protege. And it will find it is having to do deals with its international rivals so as to keep the damage to its wider interests to a minimum.

It is difficult to see how it could be otherwise. The European powers abandoned colonialism in the 1950s and 1960s not out of benevolence, but because it did not pay economically in the face of insurgent nationalist movements and changes in the structure of the world economy. European empires had been self financing at the high point of the old imperialism a century ago, with India and Ireland always paying a surplus into the British Treasury—imperial possessions were a drain on budgets by the 1950s. A decade later the US found the costs of trying to hold on to Vietnam through massive physical occupation far too excessive. This was why the Nixon administration eventually retreated from waging an all-out land war to a policy of trying to subdue the country by air strikes—and withdrew from the country when that did not work.

If the major sources of surplus value in the world are in the advanced countries, then the only real way to begin seriously to defray the costs of a high level of military expenditure would be to do what Germany did during the Second World War, and to establish occupation regimes in advanced countries which squeezed them dry. However arrogant they feel after Iraq, the apostles of the New American Century are not yet ready to do that—and mainstream US capital would put up serious opposition if they tried.

The US state cannot retreat from its occupation of Iraq, or even from its wider 'unilateralist' posturing against France, Germany and Russia. To do so would be to abandon the gains from its military gamble at the moment it seems to be winning, and to risk a cumulative loss of influence over other states and other capitalisms. Under the leadership of Cheney, Rumsfeld, Bush, Perle, Wolfowitz and the rest, it has set out on a journey from which it cannot easily turn back. Having raised the level of military expenditure, it will try to get a return on its investment by further military actions designed to increase still more its leverage over the other major players in the international system. But the outcome will never be satisfactory for US capitalism. It cannot make enough out of imperialism in crude cash terms to compensate for its expenditures in the way that the European capitalisms did a century ago. Nor can it rely, as it could during the Second World War and the early years of the Cold War, on military spending allowing it to prosper with a prolonged boom. The level of spending required to push the economy back into such a boom would, even more than in the Reagan years, damage US market competitiveness.

As John K Galbraith has pointed out, the US dependence on huge imports means its position 'much more closely resembles the great powers in Europe in 1914 that that of America in 1939... To finance either a major military or a major domestic economic effort or both on world capital markets could very well unhinge the dollar and shift the balance of financial power—presumably to Europe'.[153] But it cannot abandon its military commitments without damaging the hegemony which its multinational corporations need to protect their interests in an increasingly tumultuous world.

For these reasons, the US triumphant remains the US weak. The splits with the other powers will continue, even though they will alternate between defiant gestures and grovelling actions. There will also be recurrent splits within the US political establishment and ruling class as the Bush magic fails to transmute military self glorification into the humdrum business of making bigger profits.

None of this will make the world less barbarous. Those who have tasted blood will want more, and we can expect further aggressive wars. But it will make it easier to build the forces of resistance to them worldwide. They won a war in which they enjoyed a 30 or 40 to one military superiority. We were part of the biggest anti-imperialist mobilisations that the world has ever seen. And that experience will be there, as underlying weakness shows.

Notes

1   M Hardt, *The Guardian*, 18 December 2002.
2   B Cassen, 'On the Attack', *New Left Review*, January/February 2003, pp52-53.
3   V I Lenin, *Imperialism: The Highest Stage of Capitalism* (London, 1933), pp10-11.
4   Ibid, p108.
5   Ibid, pp20-21.
6   Ibid, pp24-25.
7   Ibid, p26.
8   Ibid, p60.
9   Ibid, pp68-69.
10   Ibid, p69.
11   K Kautsky, quoted ibid, section 7: 'Imperialism, as a Special Stage of Capitalism'.
12   Ibid.
13   N I Bukharin, *Imperialism and World Economy*, ch 10: 'Reproduction of the Processes of Concentration and Centralisation of Capital on a World Scale', available on www.marxists.org/archive/bukharin/works/1917/imperial/10.htm
14   His major work, *Imperialism and World Economy*, did not appear in any English edition between the 1920s and 1970, while the first English edition of his subsequent *Economics of the Transformation Period* (with marginal notes by Lenin) was not published until 50 years after it was written. See *Economics of the Transformation Period* (New York, 1971).
15   Figures From H Feis, *Europe: The World's Banker, 1879-1914*, quoted in M Kidron, 'Imperialism: The Highest Stage but One', in *International Socialism* 9 (first series), p18.

16 The argument and the figures for this are provided by M Barratt Brown, *The Economics of Imperialism* (Harmondsworth, 1974), p195.
17 For a longer discussion of the economic connections between the two changes, see C Harman, *Explaining the Crisis* (London 1984), pp52-53.
18 C Harman, *A People's History of the World* (London 1999), p397.
19 J A Hobson, *Imperialism: A Study* (New York, 1902), www.econlib.org/library/YPDBooks/Hobson/hbsnImp5.html#
20 Ibid, part 1, ch 4.
21 M Salvadori, *Karl Kautsky and the Socialist Revolution, 1880-1938* (London, 1979), p171.
22 Ibid, p172.
23 Ibid.
24 All quotes are from K Kautsky, 'Imperialism and the War', *International Socialist Review* (November 1914), available on www.marxists.org/archive/kautsky/works/1910s/war.html
25 See Kautsky's review of Hilferding's *Finance Capital*: K Kautsky, 'Finance-Capital and Crises', *Social Democrat*, London, vol 15, 1911, available on www.marxists.org/archive/kautsky/works/1910s/finance.htm
26 R Hilferding, *Finance Capital* (London, 1981), p225.
27 Ibid, p225.
28 Ibid, p304.
29 Ibid, p325.
30 Ibid, p226.
31 K Kautsky, 'Finance-Capital and Crises', op cit.
32 R Hilferding, op cit, p294.
33 W Smaldone, *Rudolf Hilferding: The Tragedy of a German Social Democrat* (Illinois, 1996).
34 V I Lenin, introduction to *Imperialism: The Highest Stage of Capitalism*, op cit.
35 Ibid, ch 3, 'Finance Capital and the Financial Oligarchy'.
36 Ibid.
37 T Cliff, 'The Nature of Stalinist Russia', in T Cliff, *Marxist Theory after Trotsky* (London, 2003), pp116-120.
38 Ibid, p117.
39 N I Bukharin, *Imperialism and World Economy*, op cit, p114.
40 Ibid, p118.
41 Ibid, p104.
42 N I Bukharin, *Economics of the Transformation Period* (New York, 1971), p36.
43 N I Bukharin, *Imperialism and World Economy*, op cit, pp124-127.
44 N I Bukharin, 'Address to the Fourth Congress of the Comintern', in *Bulletin of Fourth Congress*, vol 1, Moscow, 24 November 1922, p7.
45 V I Lenin, 'The Discussion On Self-Determination Summed Up', *Collected Works* (Moscow, 1964), vol 22, section 10: 'The Irish Rebellion of 1916'.
46 For the impact in China see, for instance, Chesnais' magnificent *The Chinese Labor Movement*.
47 V I Lenin, *Imperialism: The Highest Stage of Capitalism*, op cit, ch 4, 'Export of Capital'.
48 Leon Trotsky spelt out the argument about industrial development in 1928: 'Capitalism...equalises the economic and cultural levels of the most advanced and most backward countries. Without this main process, it would be impossible to conceive...the diminishing gap between India and Britain' (Leon Trotsky, *The Third International After Lenin* (New York, 1957), p209).
49 J Degras (ed), *The Comintern, 1939-43, Documents*, vol 2 (London, 1971), p527.
50 Ibid, p528.
51 Ibid, p529.

52   Ibid, p534.
53   R Debray, 'Problems of Revolutionary Strategy in Latin America', *New Left Review* 45, September-October 1967.
54   Michael Barratt Brown concludes, after a detailed examination of the evidence, 'The important point in that the underdeveloped lands gained in volume terms and in unit values from 1900 right up to 1930' (M Barratt Brown, *The Economics of Imperialism* (Harmondsworth, 1974), p248).
55   I Roxborough, *Theories of Underdevelopment* (London, 1979), pp27-32.
56   Leon Trotsky showed some confusion over these matters in an article he wrote about Latin America while in exile in Mexico. He refers to Brazil under the Vargas government as both 'semi-fascist' and a 'semi-colony'. See L Trotsky, *Escritos Latinoamericanos* (Buenos Aires, 1999).
57   V I Lenin, *Imperialism: The Highest Stage of Capitalism*, op cit, section 7, 'Imperialism, as a Special Stage of Capitalism'.
58   C Harman, *Explaining the Crisis* (London, 1984), p71.
59   For an account of these tensions, see G Kolko, *The Politics of War* (New York, 1968).
60   F Sternberg, *Capitalism and Socialism on Trial* (London, 1950), p538.
61   Figures given in O G Wichel, *Survey of Current Business* (August 1980), p18.
62   For details, see C Harman, *Class Struggles in Eastern Europe 1945-83* (London, 1988), pp42-49.
63   Calculation by Alan Winters, contained in *Financial Times*, 16 November 1987.
64   *New York Times*, 5 July 1950, quoted in T N Vance, 'The Permanent War Economy', *New International*, January-February 1951.
65   For graphs showing levels of US arms expenditure, see www.albany.edu/~fordham/dec12.pdf
66   See various calculations given in C Harman, *Explaining the Crisis*, op cit, p80.
67   For an explanation of this in terms of Marxist theory, see ibid, pp81-82.
68   M Kidron, 'Imperialism: The Highest Stage but One', in *International Socialism*, first series, no 9, 1962, available on www.marxists.de/theory/kidron/imperial.htm
69   J Stopford and S Strange, *Rival States, Rival Firms* (Cambridge, 1991), p16.
70   All figures are from M J Twomey, 'Patterns of Foreign Investment', in JH Coastsworth and A M Taylor, *Latin America and the World Economy since 1800*, p188.
71   As Roxborough points out, Gunder Frank 'never claimed to be a Marxist' (I Roxborough, op cit, p49).
72   P Baran, *The Political Economy of Growth* (Harmondsworth, 1973), p399.
73   Ibid, p416.
74   A Gunder Frank, *Capitalism and Underdevelopment in Latin America* (Harmondsworth, 1971), pp35-36.
75   Despite Baran's preparedness to criticise certain features of Stalin's rule, he quoted Stalin himself favourably and repeated Stalinist lies about the USSR's agricultural performance and living standards. See, for example, P Baran, op cit, p441. Contrast Baran's treatment with the critical, scientific assessment of Soviet figures to be found in Tony Cliff's writings of the 1940s and 1950s, for instance 'The Nature of Stalinist Russia' (written in 1947), in T Cliff, *Marxist Theory after Trotsky*, op cit, pp116-120.
76   For discussions of the role Britain played in Argentina see, for instance, R Miller, *Britain and Argentina in the Nineteenth Century* (New York, 1993); R Gravil, *The Anglo-Argentine Connection 1900-1939* (Boulder and London 1985); R Hara, 'Landowning Bourgeoisie or Business Bourgeoisie', *Journal of Latin American Studies*, 34 (August 2002), pp587-623; D C M Platt and G di Tella (eds), *Argentina, Australia and Canada: Studies in Comparative Development* (London, 1985); M A Garcia, *Peronismo: desarrollo económico y lucha de clases en*

Argentina (Espluges de Llobregat, 1980) (the chapter on Peronism of this important work is available on the webpage http://humano.ya.com/flasheva/miguel.htm).

77 M Kidron, 'Memories of development', *New Society*, 4 March 1971, reprinted in M Kidron, *Capitalism and Theory* (London, 1974), p173.

78 See for instance E Mandel, *Europe Versus America* (London, 1970).

79 According to OECD calculations in the late 1970s.

80 *Financial Times*, World Banking Survey, 22 May 1986.

81 Ibid.

82 *Financial Times*, International Capital Markets Survey, 21 April 1987.

83 J Burke and G Epstein, 'Threat Effects of the Internationalisation of Production', Political Economy Research Institute working paper series, no 15 (University of Massachusetts, 2001).

84 UNCTAD, 'Overview', *World Investment Report 2001*, table 1.

85 J Burke and G Epstein, op cit.

86 Ibid.

87 Figures from US Bureau of Economic Analysis website.

88 H Skytta, *The European Union and World Trade*, Speakers Bureau, November 2002.

89 J Burke and G Epstein, op cit.

90 Table based on figures in P Hirst and G Thompson, *Globalisation in Question* (London, 1996), pp91-94.

91 W Ruigrok and R van Tulder, *The Logic of International Restructuring* (London, 1995), p156.

92 Figures given in www.jil.go.jp/emm/vol.28/labornegotiation.htm

93 W Ruigrok and R van Tulder, op cit, pp157-158.

94 M F Hijtjes, R Olie and U Glunk, 'Board Internationalisation and the Multinational Company', (Amsterdam, 2001).

95 See the Microsoft and Exxon-Mobil corporate websites.

96 Interview with Louis Schweitzer on www.renault.com/gb/groupe/strategie_pl.htm

97 Estimate from Global Anti-Counterfeiting Group, in *Financial Times*, 30 April 2002.

98 For an account of the importance of this for US corporations' exports, see R Brenner, *The Boom and the Bubble* (London, 2002), pp59-64.

99 W Ruigrok and R van Tulder, op cit, p219.

100 D Bryan, 'Global Accumulation and Accounting for National Economic Identity', *Review of Radical Political Economy* 33 (2001), pp57-77.

101 Quoted in D Halberstam, *The Best and the Brightest* (London, 1970), p78.

102 For details, see C Harman, *The Fire Last Time* (London, 1987).

103 See the graphs available on www.albany.edu/~fordham/Dec12.pdf

104 This process is well described in the first part of P Gowan, *The Global Gamble* (London and New York, 1999), pp3-240. But he has tendency to see the whole thing as planned by US governments, rather than as representing a response by them to unforeseen changes in the world system.

105 See, for instance, H Kissinger, *Diplomacy* (New York, 1994), and Z Brzezinski, *The Geostrategic Triangle* (Washington, 2001).

106 J Perlez, 'Blunt Reason For Enlarging NATO: Curbs On Germany', *New York Times*, 7 December 1997.

107 H Kissinger, op cit, p809.

108 Ibid, p813.

109 Ibid, p821.

110 Ibid, p116.

111 Z Brzezinski, op cit, p4.

112 Ibid, p29.

113   Ibid, p31.
114   Ibid, pviii.
115   On the continuity of this group and the development their approach in the 1990s, see A Callinicos, 'The Grand Strategy of the American Empire', *International Socialism* 97 (Winter 2002).
116   *Weekly Standard*, 7 September 1997.
117   Project for the New American Century, *Statement of Principle*, 7 June 1997.
118   Project for the New American Century, letter of 29 May 1998.
119   The proportion of Democrats voting for increased arms spending doubled between 1993 and 1998, although it remained lower than for Republicans: see graph on www.albany.edu/~fordham/dec12.pdf
120   See the graph for net lending by foreigners to US in *Financial Times*, 19 February 2003.
121   M Wolf, *Financial Times*, 19 February 2003.
122   Ibid.
123   This available on http://scienceforpeace.sa.utoronto.ca/New_NOOS/Presentations/ visbook.pdf
124   A J Chien, 'Iraq: Is It About Oil?', Znet, 13 October 2002.
125   Unedited transcript, Middle East Policy Council, Thirty-First Capitol Hill Conference on US Middle East Policy, 'In the Wake of War: Geo-strategy, Terrorism, Oil Markets, and Domestic Politics'.
126   M Wolf, *Financial Times*, 19 February 2003.
127   United Nations Conference on Trade and Development, *World Investment Report 2001*, p10.
128   J Burke and G Epstein, op cit, p5.
129   European Union, 'Questions Related to Our Bi-regional Partnership with Latin America and the Caribbean', on www.delbnol.ced.eu.int/sp/documentos/cumbre
130   Quote in *Financial Times*, 3 April 2003.
131   A Moravcsik, *Financial Times*, 3 April 2003.
132   Ibid.
133   G Monbiot, 'The Bottom Dollar', *The Guardian*, 22 April 2003.
134   *Financial Times*, 1 December 2002.
135   P Rogers, *The Guardian*, 13 January 2001.
136   Report by the Techint group of companies, June 2001, www.techintgroup.com/ origins/origins.html
137   *Financial Times*, 13 July 1990.
138   J Burke and G Epstein, op cit, p2.
139   Figure given by Jubilee Research in *HIPC: How the Poor are Financing the Rich*. A report from Jubilee Research at the New Economics Foundation by Romilly Greenhill and Ann Pettifor, April 2002, on www.jubilee2000uk.org/analysis/ reports/J+USA7.htm
140   'Trade Makes US Strong', www.ustrade.org/brt/myths/investment.html
141   M C Penido and D Magalhaes Prates, 'Financial Openness: The Experience of Argentina, Brazil and Mexico', *CEPAL Review* 70 (April 2000), p61.
142   Ibid, p60.
143   A Calderon and R Casilda, 'The Spanish Banks Strategy in Latin America', *CEPAL Review* 70 (April 2000), pp78-79.
144   Ibid, p79.
145   M C Penido and D Magalhaes Prates, op cit, p63.
146   F Chesnais, *La Mondialisation du Capital* (Paris, 1997), p83.
147   Figures for relative sizes of GDPs of Latin American countries and US states given in *IMF Staff Country Report 99/101*, September 1999.
148   In the case of the Venezuelan stoppage of 2002-2003, a key section of the Venezuelan ruling class were so carried away with their hatred for the Chávez

regime that they proceeded in a way which went against the immediately tactical interests of the US. The last thing it wanted was a cutback in supplies of Venezuelan oil (its third biggest source of oil imports) just as it was preparing for war against Iraq. This misinterpretation of US wishes was one reason that the attempt to remove Chávez failed, with pro-opposition newspaper columnists bemoaning the lack of greater US support from the summer of 2002 onwards.

149 *Theses, Resolutions and Manifestos of the First Four Congresses of the Communist International* (London, 1980), p80.

150 For details of the downward trend in profit rates, see R Brenner, *The Boom and the Bubble*, op cit, table 1.2, and figures 1.1, 1.2, 1.3, 1.4, 2.9, 2.10, 2.11, 10.1, 11.1. His evidence for the downward trend is all the more convincing given that he mistakenly rejects the classic Marxist 'law of the tendency of the rate of profit to fall'.

151 For a serious attempt at this, see J Tatom, 'Iraqi Oil is not America's Objective', *Financial Times*, 14 February 2003.

152 At least one pro-capitalist economist argued well before the recent war that if the military and other costs of maintaining US influence in the Middle East were taken into account, the cost of Middle East oil to the US was 'between two and five times higher than the spot price'. See N A Bailey, 'Venezuela and the United States', in L W Goodman et al (eds), *Lessons of the Venezuelan Experience* (Washington, 1995), pp391-392.

153 J K Galbraith, 'Thoughts on the War Economy', on http://utip.gov.utexas.edu/web/Jgarchive/2001/the%20economy.pdf

Daring for victory: Iraq in revolution 1946-1959

ANNE ALEXANDER

Few of the US colonial administrators now arriving to take up power in Baghdad know much of Iraq's history. They may yet pay for their ignorance. The last time the imperialist powers installed a loyal regime in Baghdad, it was overthrown by a massive revolt from below. Yet tragically, it was not Iraq's workers and peasants who benefited from the collapse of the old order. Instead, the failure of the Iraqi Communist Party (ICP) allowed the nationalists of the Ba'ath Party to seize the initiative, and ultimately take control of the state itself. With Washington's approval, the Ba'athists crushed the revolutionary hopes of the 1950s, murdering thousands of Communists in the process.[1]

The crisis in Iraq was only part of a long wave of protest, which engulfed the Middle East after the end of the Second World War. From Egypt to Iran, from Syria to Algeria, the mass movement swept the region. But just as in Iraq, it was nationalist army officers and intellectuals who captured the state at the moment of revolutionary crisis, not organised workers. And having taken power, the nationalist leaders of the 1950s succumbed to the pressures of imperialism. The great powers quickly found new means of maintaining their domination of the Middle East.

The movements of the 1940s and 1950s carry important lessons for activists today. This is the real tradition of anti-imperialism and democracy in the Middle East against the fake radicalism of the dictators and the false freedoms of US 'liberation'. The role of the organised working class in smashing apart the old colonial order has long been hidden from history, but it should inspire a new generation of socialists. These movements involved masses of workers and peasants—the poor, the dispossessed and the marginalised—in remaking the world. Ordinary people fought the police and army, and defied the might of empire in the name of freedom. Despite the failure of their leaders, the history of the national liberation movements show that change does come from below.

The Middle East at the crossroads[2]

The years following the Second World War were marked by instability and turmoil across the Middle East. As the old colonial powers retreated, the social structures they had supported since the 1920s began to crumble. Across the Middle East the 1940s and 1950s were a period of deep revolutionary crisis. The collapse of the colonial-sponsored regimes was not just the work of a handful of army officers. It was the railway workers of Baghdad and the textile workers of the Egyptian Delta, students in Cairo, Alexandria and Damascus, and peasant activists in the valley of the Nile and the hills of Kurdistan, who dealt the death blow to the old order.

A militant trade union movement emerged which began to challenge not only foreign capitalists in the name of the nation, but also local capitalists in the name of the working class. The industrial struggle fed back into the nationalist movement, where street protests were accompanied by massive waves of strikes.[3] Unrest in the cities was shadowed by a gradual breakdown of social order in the countryside. Peasant movements in Syria and Egypt began to emerge towards the end of the 1940s to challenge the pashas for control of the land.[4]

The catastrophe of Palestine played a crucial role in undermining the old order. The creation of the state of Israel in 1948 and the expulsion of hundreds of thousands of Palestinians from their homes had the effect of further radicalising the mass movement. The complete inability of the old regimes to defend the Palestinians, despite sending troops to fight the Zionists, was the final nail in the coffin.

However, despite the deep crisis and eventual collapse of the old order, it was not the working class that benefited. The Communist parties, hamstrung by Stalinist ideas of an alliance with the 'progressive national bourgeoisie', tied the fate of the working class movement to nationalist goals. Having politically disarmed the workers' movement, the Communists were then unable to resist repression by the new regimes.

A society in motion

In Iraq, the eruption of a mass anti-colonial movement was the most visible sign of the accelerating change beneath the surface of society. Two new classes—urban workers and the modern lower middle class—dominated the political organisations thrown up by the movement. Their political prominence reflected the growing role of industrial production in the Iraqi economy, and the increasing weight of a modern state bureaucracy in Iraqi society.

The Iraqi working class grew rapidly during the 1940s and 1950s. The outbreak of the Second World War stimulated the Iraqi economy—in particular domestic industrial production—by cutting off the ready supply of foreign goods. The influx of British troops provided an important market for local products, and the army directly employed a large number of Iraqis.[5] Iraqi industry experienced another growth spurt in the 1950s—between 1953 and 1958 industrial production rose by 85 percent.[6]

In particular, the explosive growth of oil production in this period created a strategically vital and technologically advanced industry which employed tens of thousands of local workers. A national strike by Iraqi oil workers, who numbered around 15,000 by 1958, had the power to choke off production in a sector which accounted for 28 percent of GNP and 61 percent of government revenues.[7] The development of a modern transport network created another powerful group of workers. The 1,200 or so workers from railway repair shops at Schalchiyyah, near Baghdad, were key: 'Stoppage of activity in this place for ten to 15 days would have brought the movement of trains in the whole of Iraq to a complete standstill'.[8]

The structure of capitalism in Iraq gave workers a decisive role in the battle against imperialism. European and US capital directly controlled large parts of the economy. The oil companies were the most obvious— and politically contentious—symbols of the domination of foreign capital. The Iraq Petroleum Company was a consortium of the world's major oil companies. British Petroleum, which controlled the reserves of neighbouring Iran, had the lion's share. Shell took around 25 percent, as did a group of the largest US oil companies. A share went to the French government and one individual—Calouste Gulbenkian—owned the rest. In 1925, Iraq's King Faisal—who owed his throne to the work of British bayonets—was prevailed upon to sign away Iraq's oil until the year 2000. The company refused to give the Iraqi government a share in the profits, instead offering royalties of four gold shillings per ton of oil.[9]

Transport and public utilities were also governed by similar 'concessionary agreements' with European capital. British companies ran Basra port and the railway system.[10] Generations of imperial civil servants had worked hard to maintain the direct domination of British and French capital in the Middle East. Now they found that these companies quickly became a focus for nationalist anger. The concessionary companies—once seen as convenient cash cows by European shareholders and government officials—brought the battle for national liberation into the workplace and proved to be a fertile training ground for a new generation of industrial activists. Railway and port workers in Iraq formed the core of the Communist Party's industrial organisation during the 1940s and 1950s.[11]

The expansion of a secular education system and the exponential growth in the government bureaucracies helped to create a small but important modern lower middle class.[12] The social crisis radicalised this layer, who provided many leaders of the Communist and nationalist movements of the time. Crucially the modern middle class found itself excluded from political power, which remained in the hands of the large landowners.[13] In Iraq this process coincided with religious and ethnic faultlines. A small secular-educated Shi'i and Kurdish middle class emerged in Iraq in the 1940s, only to find its development blocked by the continued Sunni and Arab domination of the political system.[14] For Sunnis outside the ruling class, the army provided an important vehicle for upward mobility.

The crisis of the old regime

The corrupt and repressive Hashemite monarchy was British colonialism's legacy to the people of Iraq. At the end of the First World War the first king, Faisal, had briefly created an Arab kingdom centred on Damascus, before being ejected by French troops. British advisers now lobbied for him to be offered the throne of Iraq. Creating the new Iraqi monarchy proved to be a difficult task. It took thousands of British troops and £40 million to suppress a huge uprising in 1920.[15] Unrest and nationalist agitation continued for months afterwards.

A combination of repression and bribery eventually secured Faisal's place on the throne. Iraq gained nominal independence in 1932 and a seat in the League of Nations. In reality little changed: British advisers remained firmly in power behind the scenes, and a treaty between the two governments maintained Britain's military domination of Iraq.[16] It was the negotiations over the extension of this treaty which provided the spark for a wave of mass protests across Iraq in 1948.

Even in the 1920s the social base of support for the Iraqi monarchy had been very thin. By the 1940s this layer was even more isolated, as new social forces, such as the growing working class, the urban poor and the new middle class, combined in protest at its continued domination. The government's usual answer was increased repression. Parties were banned, strikers shot down, and Communists executed in public. As early as 1946 even the British embassy was wringing its hands in despair. A report from the chancery in Baghdad to the Foreign Office noted: 'With the old gang in power this country cannot hope to progress very far'.[17]

A growing sense of social polarisation added to the tension. The cost of basic goods sky-rocketed during the 1940s, and although wages rose as the war economy expanded, they could not keep pace with the cost of living.[18] With the end of the war, jobs dependent on the British army evaporated, adding thousands to the ranks of the unemployed when prices and rents remained ruinously high. War profiteering combined with an oil boom allowed a thin layer of the elite to indulge in conspicuous consumption. The arrogance of the rich sharpened the anger of the nationalist demonstrations. In the minds of many Iraqis, the interests of their own ruling class were indistinguishable from the interests of British imperialism.

Moreover, foreign capitalists were not the only people who were getting rich. Large landowners dominated the small local ruling class. A boom in agricultural production increased the wealth and power of this tiny handful. In an effort to provide a social base for their imported monarchy, British colonial officials had played an important role in consolidating the power of this class. Changes to the property laws during the 1920s made tribal sheikhs' and politicians' fortunes overnight. The landlords had every interest in continuing to work with the colonial powers to maintain their domination of the Iraqi economy. As Phebe Marr explains: 'Iraq [was] highly dependent upon the export of two primary products—oil and agricultural products—the one controlled by foreign interests and the other by a group of wealthy landlords'.[19]

Meanwhile industrialisation, even on a small scale, pulled people out of the villages into the great urban centres. Baghdad's population doubled in size between 1922 and 1946.[20] However, many migrants did not find the work they were looking for. Instead they swelled the growing ranks of the urban poor and unemployed. 'Sarifahs'—mud-walled houses thatched with reed matting—sprang up on the outskirts of Baghdad to absorb the newcomers, who featured prominently in the crowd scenes of the crisis.[21]

However, despite the bankruptcy of the monarchy, none of Iraq's nationalist opposition parties developed a mass membership while nationalist leaders of an earlier generation often played a leading role in the repressive governments of the period.[22] In fact, as in Egypt in the same period, the nationalist movement moved quickly leftwards, drawing its leaders from precisely those new social groups which had no stake in the existing system. Iraq's political future was being decided at the level of the street, where the parliamentary parties had little influence.

Majid Khadduri sums up neatly the dilemma of the establishment after the fall of Salih Jabr's government in 1948. The leaders of the parliamentary opposition parties:

> ...*seem*[ed] *to have co-operated only to force the Jabr government to resign, but were wholly unprepared to follow up their victory and achieve power. Their weakness became the more apparent when the parties appealed to the mob (presumed to have been under their control) to stop street demonstrations; the mob would not listen to them.*[23]

The rise of the Communists

Organised Communist activity began in Iraq during the 1930s. Cells sprang up in Nasiriyyah, Basra, Baghdad and other towns. A small core of activists travelled to Moscow to enrol at the Communist University of the Toilers of the East (KUTV), a Communist Party training school.[24] The KUTV's most influential Iraqi graduate was Fahd (Yusuf Salman Yusuf), the party's secretary-general between 1941 and 1949.

Fahd's most trusted comrades were mainly drawn from a layer of working class party members. They included Zaki Basim, a tannery worker and later a clerk; Ali Shukur, a railway driver; and Ahmad Abbas, the son of a peasant, who later worked in the railway repair shops in Schalchiyyah, and then a textile factory, before finally becoming a mechanic.[25]

The rise of these men to prominent positions in the party leadership was the outward sign of a deeper shift towards systematic industrial organisation. Majid Khadduri, writing not long after the revolution of 1958, argues that Fahd's influence was decisive in achieving this change of direction: 'His significance was not so much in providing leadership for the movement—his leadership was by no means universally accepted by Iraqi Communists—but in shifting its appeal from the intellectuals to the masses'.[26]

Hanna Batatu provides a detailed account of how this was done. The Communists played a vital role in the struggle for trade union rights. The Communist Party dominated 12 of the 16 trade unions legalised between 1944 and 1945: 'the drafts of their programme were in Fahd's own handwriting'.[27] A network of members and supporters began to take shape in key industries: 'The party sought before everything to convert the railways, the port of Basra, and the oilfields into Communist fortresses'.[28]

The prominent role played by Communists in leading mass strikes in all these workplaces is a testament to the success of this strategy. According to Batatu's calculations, workers formed around 25 percent of the ICP under Fahd's leadership. Five years after his death, despite increasing government repression, they still formed around 20 percent of all known ICP members.[29]

Work among university and secondary school students brought thousands of young activists into contact with the party's ideas. Students played a crucial role in the mass protests—the signal for the uprisings of 1948 and 1952 was given by students spilling onto the streets of Baghdad. The movement of the 1940s and 1950s was a revolt led largely by young people and the party reflected this in its ranks—in 1947, 74 percent of the rank and file activists were under the age of 26.[30]

In other crucial ways the ICP came to represent the hopes of a generation. The mass movement carried in it the seeds of a challenge to the sectarian structure of Iraqi society. The interweaving of state and sect was most obvious in the historic exclusion of Iraq's Shi'i majority from the machinery of government.[31] One factor pulling Shi'is into the Communist Party during this period was growing anger at their continued oppression by the state. Shi'is made up most of the rank and file of the party and 47 percent of its leadership by 1955.[32] The influx of Shi'i members was also an expression of increasing class polarisation within the Shi'i community. Despite the appointment of two Shi'i prime ministers in 1948, ever larger numbers of young Shi'is had come to oppose not only 'the authority or actions of any one particular government, but the entire order of Iraqi society and politics'.[33]

The ICP's Kurdish members also played a prominent role in the party leadership. In Kurdistan the party began to develop a base in the countryside by taking on the local landlords, the aghas. The party supported a peasant uprising in Arbat, near Sulaymaniyyah, in 1947. The revolt exploded after the landlord, Sheikh Latif, told the villagers to give him a third of their crops, instead of the customary tenth. The ICP's support meant that the uprising, which forced a compromise from Sheikh Latif, won the backing of townspeople in Sulaymaniyyah. The peasants were no longer isolated. As David McDowell explains, 'Arbat was something of a watershed: for the first time in living memory, the peasantry had taken on the agha class, demonstrating that change was a real possibility'.[34]

Although Kurdish nationalism would revive after 1958, during the 1940s and early 1950s the Communists' support for Kurdish national rights combined with their defence of Kurdish peasants and workers meant that in many areas of Kurdistan the ICP could count on much greater support than the nationalist Kurdistan Democratic Party (KDP). In fact, the Communist Party pulled the KDP leftwards, marginalising traditional leaders such as Mulla Mustafa Barzani, father of today's KDP leader, Mas'ud Barzani.[35]

Out of all the Communist parties in the Arab world, the ICP came closest to building a mass revolutionary party. By 1947, the organisation counted around 1,800 members—no mean feat for an underground party.[36]

Under the impact of repression, membership levels had fallen to around 500 on the eve of the 1958 revolution, but the fall of the old regime opened the floodgates. Police figures put the number of party members at 25,000 at the height of the ICP's influence in 1958-1959. The party's daily paper was selling 23,000 copies. In addition the party dominated the League for the Defence of Women's Rights with its 25,000 members, the Iraqi Democratic Youth Federation which claimed 84,000 members by mid-June 1959, the Partisans of Peace with around 250,000 members and the General Federation of Trade Unions which claimed to organise 275,000 workers and artisans by 8 July 1959.[37] The ICP also dominated—thanks to its growing influence in the army and the reserves—the militia forces of the People's Resistance, a semi-official paramilitary body, which counted 25,000 members by 1959.

Hanna Batatu points out that this exponential growth in membership carried with it its own dangers, as thousands flocked to a party which seemed to have the favour of the new leaders of the country.[38] However, even five years later, on the eve of the Ba'ath Party coup of 1963, a local Communist organiser estimated there were 5,000 members in Baghdad alone.[39] The same year, Iraqi police files listed the names of over 200 party members in Basra workplace party branches.[40] As Batatu explains:

> In 1963, when the boot was on the other foot, the Ba'ath was never able at any time to bring together one third of the crowds that the Communists attracted in 1959... In such poor and strictly labouring places such as Al-Thawrah town or Tabbat al-Akrad on Al-Rasafah side, and Kreimat or Al-Shawwakah districts on the Karkh side of Baghdad, a thrill of hope greeted their rise to great influence.[41]

The ICP's weakness lay in its politics rather than its organisation. Having achieved 'great influence', through its pivotal role in the nationalist and democratic struggle, the party was incapable of offering independent leadership to the workers' movement at the point of crisis. The party leadership maintained that the struggle in Iraq would have to pass through two stages—first a national and democratic revolution against the colonial power and its local allies, and only then could workers raise the question of social revolution.[42] As a result, when the party faced a choice between challenging the Free Officers' leader, Abd'al-Karim Qassem for power in 1959, and thus breaking their alliance with the nationalist forces he represented, the ICP chose to back away from the brink. Such a step would have required not only a break from decades of Stalinist orthodoxy, but also a break with Moscow as well as setting the Iraqi Revolution on a collision course with Western imperialism. The results of the ICP's retreat were tragic—within a year the party had been forced back into the underground, hundreds of Communists were killed and the stage was set for the rise of the Ba'ath Party.

From uprising to revolution

Iraq's historical vocabulary is rich in the language of protest. Al-Wathba, al-Intifada, al-Thawra—all these words make an appearance during the 13-year period of crisis. 'Al-Wathba' (the Leap) comes first: 1948's mass urban rebellion against the old regime and the British. The revolt was crushed. Communist leaders died on the gallows and the party was forced underground. 'Al-Intifada' (the Uprising) followed: student protests of 1952 marked the mass movement's return to the streets. 1958 saw the outbreak of revolution, 'al-Thawra'.

The first great explosion of protest came as the Iraqi government entered negotiations over the revision of the Anglo-Iraqi Treaty of 1930. Iraq's independence from Britain at the end of the mandate in 1932 had little substance while the treaty remained in force. Iraqi politicians promised to accept British 'guidance' in matters of foreign policy and the RAF controlled Iraq's key air bases. Attempts to renegotiate the treaty in 1948 triggered 'al-Wathba'—a massive urban uprising led by students, workers and the urban poor. However, as Hanna Batatu describes, the protests had a sharp edge of class anger:

> *It was the social subsoil of Baghdad in revolt against hunger and unequal burdens. It was students and Schalchiyyah* [railway] *workers braving machine guns on the Ma'mun Bridge and dying for their ideas.*[43]

The central demand of the protests was the cancellation of the treaty and when the government announced the new terms—which amounted to the treaty's extension, rather than its abrogation—huge demonstrations broke out in Baghdad.[44] Led by school and university students, the protests were quickly radicalised by brutal repression. On 26 January 1948, the police fired on unarmed demonstrators, killing many:

> *The demonstrators advanced, seemingly determined to cross* [the bridge] *in spite of any losses. For an instant the police, losing some of their assurance, hesitated. A few minutes later, however, a volley of shots burst forth. Only a 15 year old girl, Adawiyyah al-Falaki, who carried a banner and marched at the head of the column, crossed unscathed.*[45]

The protests scored an early success. Salih Jabr, Iraq's first Shi'i prime minister, was forced from office and the Iraqi government refused to endorse the treaty he had signed.

What was new about this movement was not its desperate courage, but its core of working class militants. The uprising of January 1948 followed more than two years of rising industrial struggle. In 1946 an important strike by oil workers in Kirkuk played an important role in radicalising the movement. Iraq Petroleum Company workers' confidence to take on the government and the company reflected a growing sense of militancy in the trade union movement.

As the huge street protests of 1948 subsided, major strikes continued. Railway workers struck in March and April, while postal workers went out in April and May.[46] In April the oil workers of the Iraq Petroleum Company struck again, demanding wage rises of between 25 percent and 40 percent.[47] The Communist Party played a key role in the organisation of the strike, which centred on the K3 pumping station. The strike committee organised round the clock picketing, marshalling 3,000 strikers so efficiently that production completely stopped. As one of the strike's leaders put it later, 'In a word, the dictatorship of the proletariat was established at K3 on 23 April, if the comparison is apt'.[48]

Attempting to starve the strikers back to work, the company and the government eventually cut off food and water to the pumping station, which was surrounded by hundreds of miles of desert. In response, the workers organised a march on Baghdad, 250 kilometres away. Although they were finally stopped and arrested short of their destination, the 'Great March' of the K3 workers quickly became the stuff of legend.[49]

The relationship between the nationalist and the class struggle was a key factor in maintaining the dynamic of mass protest, as Marion Farouk-Sluglett and Peter Sluglett describe:

Almost all manifestations of opposition by organised labour during the 1940s and 1950s tended to combine claims for higher wages and better living conditions with the struggle for national independence, and it was often against British-owned and British-controlled concerns that the strikes and demonstrations were concentrated. This made the labour movement both more articulate and more effective than either its numbers, its cohesion, or its apparent lack of economic muscle might suggest.[50]

The demands of the movement reflected the coalescence of the anti-colonial, democratic and economic struggles: the repudiation of the treaty with Britain, an investigation into the repression of the demonstrations, dissolution of parliament and the calling of new elections, democratic freedoms, freedom of political parties to organise, and an immediate improvement in food supplies.[51]

The outbreak of war in Palestine added to the tension. Protests in solidarity with the Palestinians had been growing in strength during the previous two years. The League Against Zionism, which was led by Jewish members of the Communist Party, had organised many of the earlier protests. In 1948 however, the Communists were temporarily disoriented by the USSR's recognition of the state of Israel. At the same time the government launched a severe crackdown, arresting hundreds of activists, and eventually executing Fahd and other Communist leaders in January 1949.

After a brief lull in the early 1950s, the movement re-emerged with the Intifada, or uprising, of 1952. External events were by now adding to the pressure on the old regime. The nationalisation of Iran's oil by prime minister Muhammad Mossadeq in 1951 and Nasser's rise to power in Egypt helped the re-emergence of the nationalist movement. The announcement of land and social reform in Egypt acted as a spur to the movement in Iraq.[52] In response to growing pressure from below, Nuri Sa'id, many-times prime minister and a key figure in the old regime, announced that his Constitutional Union Party was calling for the reform of the electoral system.

A crack had opened in the walls of the establishment, and the mass movement surged through the gap once again. Student strikes over local issues quickly turned into mass demonstrations calling for direct, free elections. Workers joined the protests, which retained a hard anti-imperialist edge:

[On 22 November] *joined by workers from the Kazimayn factories who happened to have a half-day holiday, the demonstrators broke into the US Information Service offices and burned its papers and books, and set fire to the offices of the **Iraq Times** and BOAC. They also assaulted a police station, set fire to it and killed four of the policemen inside.*[53]

The government quickly reacted by declaring martial law and banning all political parties. The regent abandoned any pretence of democracy to rule by decree. Repression did gain the old regime a breathing space of a few years, although it did not prevent the resumption of Communist activities, with the founding of the Partisans of Peace movement. The Communists also attempted to bring together a joint 'National Front' with the nationalist parties, Istiqlal (Independence) and the National Democrats.[54]

By the mid-1950s discontent was also spreading in the army. The Suez Crisis radicalised a whole generation of officers who were inspired by the success of Nasser in Egypt. The foundation of the anti-Soviet Baghdad Pact in 1955 also pushed many towards rebellion. However the nationalist officers were still a small minority inside the army, two groups of maybe

200 people in total.[55] In the event, this handful of men proved sufficient to finish off the Iraqi monarchy. On 14 July 1958 the Free Officers group launched a coup. Army units marched on the royal palace where the king and the crown prince were killed. Nuri Sa'id was hacked to death by an angry crowd as he tried to flee, disguised as a woman.

The monarchy had come to an end. A few rounds of shelling had sufficed to shake it down. Except for the feeble resistance of the guard at Nuri's house, not a hand had been lifted in its defence.[56]

The Free Officers in power

Far from ending the revolutionary process, the Free Officers' coup marked the beginning of a deeper crisis. The huge demonstrations which greeted the news of the coup of July 1958 set the pattern for the next year. Throughout this period the Communists and their allies dominated the streets of the major cities. By April 1959 some accounts put the numbers on Communist-led demonstrations as high as a million, a phenomenally high level of popular mobilisation for a country of around 6.5 million inhabitants.[57]

The Free Officers were in no position to lead this mass movement, unlike the Communists who had a network of experienced activists spanning the country. The officers' movement was small, politically inexperienced and divided. The new leaders of Iraq lacked a concrete programme of their own, and had to relate to the mass movement through others. As Marion Farouk-Sluglett and Peter Sluglett argue, the army officers who led the coup were not a cohesive body:

Those in power lacked both experience and a shared ideology, with the result that fundamental issues of principle, such as who was in command, and what form of governmental and political system should be adopted, remained unresolved. The parallel with Egypt in the first few months after July 1952 is striking.[58]

The Free Officers faced their first challenge from the left within a few days of taking power. As the monarchy came crashing down, Communist Party activists organised armed resistance cells across Baghdad. Abd'al-Karim Qassem, Iraq's new president, and the dominant figure in the Free Officers, quickly passed a law forbidding the creation of armed groups outside the state. However, Qassem's lack of a political base of his own pushed him into authorising the creation of the 'People's Resistance Force' in August 1958—essentially the Communists' resistance cells under another name. The Communist Party dominated the new body, which enrolled 11,000 young men and women within a few weeks of its founding.[59]

As the political crisis gathered pace, the signs of social revolution followed in its wake. New laws cut rents by 20 percent, the price of bread dropped by a third, and the eight-hour day was established. Labourers' wages rose by as much as 50 percent in the first year of the new republic.[60] These changes were a direct response to the growing confidence of organised workers. Although the trade unions were not formally legalised until 1959, by the evening of 14 July 1958 trade union activists were meeting to reconstitute union committees and reorganise their underground networks. The dominant force in the trade unions was once again the Communist Party, which won the leadership of most of the legal trade unions in early 1959. [61]

The countryside saw a period of intensifying pressure from below combined with reform from above. Qassem limited the power of the big landowners and organised the redistribution of thousands of acres of land to the peasants. The land reform barely kept pace with the radicalisation in the countryside. In Kut and Amarah, peasants began to sack the sheikhs' estates and seize the land for themselves.[62]

Events outside Iraq contributed to the growing sense of crisis. Gamal Abd'al-Nasser was locked in a bitter struggle with the Communist Party in Syria, following the union of Syria and Egypt in February 1958. Nasser was revered as the hero who had defied the old colonial powers over the Suez Canal in 1956, and he had moved closer to the Soviet Union, despite his persecution of the Communists in Egypt.[63] As soon as the Free Officers seized power, radical nationalists including the Ba'ath Party launched a campaign to unite Iraq with Nasser's United Arab Republic (UAR).

Neither Qassem, who had no desire to hand the presidency of Iraq to Nasser, nor the Communists, who argued that joining the UAR would mean the end of Iraq's hard-won democratic freedoms, supported the demand for total unity. The ICP organised huge demonstrations acclaiming Qassem as 'sole leader' of the Iraqi Revolution, hoping to build his support as a counterweight to Nasser.[64] When Qassem clashed with his vice-president, Abd'al-Salam Aref, who supported closer relations with the UAR, the Communists threw their weight squarely behind Qassem, although Aref called for the nationalisation of the Iraqi oil industry.[65]

In September Qassem removed Aref from power, and by November the former vice-president was on trial for his life. The foreign press interpreted Aref's fall from grace as a sign of the growing power of the Communists—journalists were soon telling their readers, 'Iraq Goes Red'.[66] Anxious talk of a 'Red Fertile Crescent' reverberated in the corridors of the State Department in Washington. US marines had already been sent to Lebanon to prop up the right wing Maronite president,

Camille Chamoun, in July 1958. US warships prowled the Gulf, while the Pentagon declared a nuclear alert.[67]

Local and international tensions intersected in Mosul in March 1959. The oil-rich city in northern Iraq had a reputation for social conservatism— Communist organisation was weaker in Mosul than in Baghdad or Basra. Mosul's political temper, combined with the city's closeness to the Syrian border, made it a likely target for nationalist officers who opposed Qassem and supported Nasser. By early 1959 rumours that the Mosul garrison was planning a coup against Qassem were beginning to circulate. In response, the Communist-led Partisans of Peace called a huge rally for 6 March. Around a quarter of a million people marched through the streets of Mosul that day, once again under the slogan 'No leader but Abd'al-Karim Qassem!'

As the last of the marchers were leaving the city the next day, fighting broke out between supporters of the Ba'ath Party and the Communists, providing the trigger for the expected coup, which was backed by the UAR. The rebellion was eventually crushed by the People's Resistance and troops loyal to Qassem, but not before the fighting had spread along the ethnic and religious faultlines in Mosul. Yet, as Hanna Batatu points out, the overwhelming divide in the conflict was class:

> *Arab soldiers clung not to the Arab officers, but to the Kurdish soldiers. The landed chieftains of Kurdish al-Gargariyyah sided with the landed chieftains of Arab Shammar...the poor and the labourers of the Arab Muslim quarters... stood shoulder to shoulder with the Kurdish and Aramean peasants against the Arab Muslim landlords.*[68]

As Iraq slid towards civil war, the CP mobilised hundreds of thousands in a demonstration on 1 May in Baghdad. Protesters called on Qassem to give the ICP a seat in the government. However, when he refused, the ICP was ill-prepared. This was the moment of real crisis— would the ICP openly challenge Qassem for power? The party issued a statement affirming that the ICP would continue to place 'its entire energies and forces at the disposal of the government of the revolution, in an unconditional manner, for the defence of the republic against threats and against the dangers of plots and aggression'.[69]

The final blows were struck in Kirkuk in July 1959. Qassem relented and allowed ICP supporters a place in his cabinet, although this turned out to be a meaningless victory. While he welcomed them as cabinet ministers on the one hand, Qassem was busy organising a purge of ICP supporters from the army.[70] Violence in Kirkuk on the eve of the anniversary of the revolution provided the opportunity for a thorough crackdown. The Turcoman minority, which had traditionally dominated the political life of

Kirkuk, was beginning to face a challenge from a Kurdish-dominated ICP. Fighting broke out over the route of the procession to mark the first anniversary of the revolution. Dozens were killed, most of them Turcomans. A wave of arrests of ICP activists followed, while the party leadership wavered. Party leaders criticised the Mosul events and disowned those implicated in the violence.[71]

This was followed by a comprehensive attempt to break the ICP. Qassem legalised a tiny rival faction in place of the real ICP and mounted an attack on the ICP leadership of the trade unions. Party publications were banned and ICP activists were targeted by nationalist hit squads. The Communists' supporters in government were dropped from the cabinet one by one.[72]

Despite a brief respite in the autumn of 1959, the ICP's influence continued to ebb away. The Ba'ath Party grew more confident. A young Ba'athist activist, Saddam Hussein, took part in an attempt on Qassem's life in 1959. Although the attempt failed, within four years the Ba'athists were able to overthrow Qassem and massacre thousands of Communist activists, foreshadowing General Pinochet's bloodbath in Chile by a decade.

Conclusion

Why did the Iraqi Communists come so close to power, and yet still fail? A crucial role was played by the Soviet leadership. In 1959 an emissary arrived from Moscow to tell the ICP's leadership that they could expect no help from the USSR if they seized power. However, despite this outside pressure, when the ICP's politburo debated the possibility of breaking with Qassem, a minority were in favour of 'daring for victory' and taking power.[73] The problem they faced was that throughout 1958, the party had made no political preparations for such a struggle. The party mobilised hundreds of thousands of workers and peasants under the slogans of national unity, rather than behind their own class demands. Rather than fight to increase the social content of the nationalist struggle, the Communists generally worked to smooth over cracks in the cross-class alliance. When Abd'al-Salam Aref raised the possibility of nationalising Iraq's oil industry, it was the pro-Communist minister of economy, Ibrahim Kubba, who reassured the multinationals that their investments were in safe hands.[74]

In the eyes of the party leadership, the Iraqi Revolution of 1958 was a bourgeois-democratic revolution, not a prelude to socialist revolution. This was why the party pinned its hopes on influencing Qassem, rather than preparing to seize power. The limited gains of the republic had to be preserved at any cost. In November 1958 the ICP attempted to revive its alliance with the nationalist parties, even though its erstwhile partners, the nationalists and the Ba'athists, were moving to the right.

Viewed from the perspective of Iraq alone, the Communists appeared to have little choice but to maintain their alliance with Qassem and the nationalist officers. Iraq's small working class, on its own, could not set about building a socialist society. However, as Trotsky realised long ago in Russia, the crucial factor was not the absolute size of the working class, but the economic and political links between the economies of the 'developing world' and the heart of the capitalist system. Events in Iraq were part of a much wider pattern of anti-colonial revolt and working class struggle, which had the potential to develop into a systematic challenge to the capitalist system. This potential existed despite the original aims of much of the anti-colonial movement, which focused on the issues of national liberation and democracy. Where the working class, rather than the bourgeoisie, played the leading role in the fight for national liberation, anti-colonial revolt carried the seeds of socialist revolution.[75]

The revolution in Iraq would not have been possible without the crisis in the region as a whole. In particular, events in Egypt, where the mass movement had already destroyed the old regime as early as 1952, played a key role in the development of the movement in Iraq. Nasser's rise to power, and in particular his defiance of Britain, France and Israel during the Suez Crisis of 1956, played an important part in radicalising officers in the Iraqi army.[76] The success of the national liberation movement in Egypt also increased the pressure on Britain, making it far more difficult for it to reassert its control of Iraq.

The influence of Egypt was also felt in a deeper way. Although the workers' movement in Egypt was unable to take political advantage of the crisis by seizing control of the state, the organised working class was instrumental in the destruction of the old regime.[77] The fall of the Egyptian monarchy in July 1952 owed as much to the textile workers of Mahalla al-Kubra and Shubra al-Khayma as it did to Nasser's Free Officers. Although Nasser attempted to break the workers' movement in Egypt by repression in the summer of 1952, he was unable to completely tame the trade unions. Strikes and workers' protests continued into the mid-1950s. In fact, the need to offer a programme of social reform that would meet the expectations of the mass movement pushed Nasser further towards a confrontation with imperialism.[78] State-led national development, and in particular control of key assets like the Suez Canal, was crucial to Nasser's strategy. So the Suez Crisis—which played such an important role in destablising the old regime in Iraq—also had its roots in the class struggle in Egypt.

A victory for the Iraqi working class had the potential to give confidence to workers' struggles right across the Middle East. It would certainly have brought about a sharp conflict with Nasser, but it could also have increased pressure on the Egyptian Free Officers' regime by reawakening the Egyptian workers' movement. Iraqi workers would have also found allies in Syria where the trade union movement was fighting Nasser's attempts to impose state control following Egyptian-Syrian unification in 1958. It was the sectors of the Syrian economy which were most closely linked to Iraq which provided the militant core of the Syrian trade union movement during this period. The Iraq Petroleum Company workers in Syria played a central role in the struggles of the 1950s and 1960s.

The threat of imperialist intervention was a powerful factor in pushing the leadership of the ICP away from confrontation with Qassem. After the coup of July 1958, British paratroopers landed in Amman to defend King Hussein from his own disgruntled officers. US troops massed on the Turkish border with Iraq.[79] However, they did not intervene to restore the Iraqi monarchy. It was not until 1967 that the US's new client state, Israel, felt militarily and politically strong enough to launch a military strike on the key Arab states.

Broadening the struggle in Iraq beyond the limits set by nationalism would have deepened and strengthened the mass movement. The Communists in Iraq found out to their cost that while the revolution remained within those limits it could neither preserve its democratic character, nor offer effective resistance to imperialism. Qassem's attack on the Communists was followed eventually by a Ba'athist coup. Once the mass movement ebbed away, Qassem's isolation was exposed. Once in power, the Ba'ath Party proved far more attentive to the interests of imperialism than its predecessors, despite its rhetoric about 'socialism' and 'Arab unity'.

Examining the events of 1958 is not an exercise in nostalgia. All of the questions thrown up by Iraq's revolutionary crisis are still being asked in the Middle East today. What is the key force in the struggle against imperialism? How is the fight for national liberation related to the struggle against capitalism? How can the ordinary people of the region defeat both their own repressive rulers and the imperialist powers? The mass protests in solidarity with the Palestinians in 2002 and the wave of demonstrations against war on Iraq in 2003 show that a new generation in the Middle East is finding its voice in the streets. The lesson of the 1940s and 1950s must be that both workers' organisation and revolutionary leadership play the crucial role in turning nationalist and democratic demands into a movement which can challenge the imperial order as a whole.

Notes

I would like to thank Dave Renton and John Rose for comments on the draft of this article. I have relied heavily on Hanna Batatu's monumental study of this period, *The Old Social Classes and the Revolutionary Movements of Iraq* (Princeton, 1978), for much of the detail. References are given throughout the text, but anyone interested in the history of the Iraqi working class movement should read it in full.

1 Peter Sluglett and Marion Farouk-Sluglett describe the killings and arrests of Communists following the Ba'athist coup of 1963 as a 'closely co-ordinated campaign'. They add, 'It is almost certain that those who carried out the raid on suspects' homes were working from lists supplied to them. Precisely how these lists had been compiled is a matter of conjecture, but it is certain that some of the Ba'athist leaders were in touch with American intelligence networks' (P Sluglett and M Farouk-Sluglett, *Iraq Since 1958* (London, 1990), p86).

2 For an overview of the early part of this period, see T Cliff, 'The Middle East at the Crossroads', in *Neither Washington nor Moscow* (London, 1982), pp11-23.

3 Joel Beinin and Zachary Lockman provide one of the best accounts of the history of this period in Egypt in *Workers on the Nile: Nationalism, Communism, Islam and the Egyptian Working Class, 1882-1954* (Princeton, 1987). For the history of Iraq, see H Batatu, op cit.

4 G Baer, *Studies in the Social History of Modern Egypt* (Chicago, 1969), p102 and T Petran, *Syria* (London, 1972), p101.

5 P Sluglett and M Farouk-Sluglett, op cit, p38.

6 P Marr, *The Modern History of Iraq* (Boulder, 1985), p132.

7 Ibid, p130.

8 H Batatu, op cit, p617.

9 A Sampson, *The Seven Sisters* (London, 1975), pp83-84.

10 H Batatu, op cit, p617.

11 Ibid, p617.

12 P Marr, op cit, p140.

13 T Cliff, 'The Middle East at the Crossroads', op cit, pp15-17.

14 Y Nakkash, *The Shi'is of Iraq* (Princeton, 1994), p133.

15 S H Longrigg, *Iraq 1900-1950* (Oxford, 1953), p123.

16 Under the renegotiated treaty Iraq's principal air bases, Habbaniyah and Shu'ayba, were to be run jointly by the RAF and the Iraqi Air Force. See M Khadduri, *Independent Iraq 1932-1958* (London,1960), pp262-265.

17 Chancery, Baghdad, to Eastern Department, Foreign Office, 16 July 1946, FO 371/52315/E 7045, quoted in P Sluglett and M Farouk-Sluglett, op cit, p309.

18 P Sluglett and M Farouk-Sluglett, op cit, p40.

19 P Marr, op cit, p136.

20 P Sluglett and M Farouk-Sluglett, op cit, p38.

21 H Batatu, op cit, p551.

22 For example, a Shi'a leader of the 1920 insurrection against Britain, Muhammad al-Sadr, was chosen by the regent to head a government charged with putting down the uprising of 1948 (H Batatu, op cit, p557).

23 M Khadduri, op cit, p270.

24 H Batatu, op cit, pp411-414.

25 Ibid, pp508-509.

26 M Khadduri, op cit, p360.

27 H Batatu, op cit, p605.

28 Ibid, p617.

29 Ibid, pp1169, 1204.

30 Ibid, p648.

31 Y Nakkash, op cit, p127.

32 Ibid, p133.

33 Ibid.

34 D McDowell, *A Modern History of the Kurds* (London, 2000), p297.

35   See ibid, pp298-299 for an account of the KDP's leftward shift.
36   H Batatu, op cit, p1177.
37   Ibid, p897.
38   Ibid, p897.
39   Ibid, p1213.
40   Ibid, p1215.
41   Ibid, p899.
42   M S Agwani, *Communism in the Arab East* (Bombay, 1969), p117.
43   H Batatu, op cit, p545.
44   The renegotiated treaty was not seen as a great improvement on the original by most Iraqis. In the event of war 'or a menace of hostilities', the King of Iraq was required to 'invite' British forces into the country. Aneurin Bevan, for the British government, seemed surprised at the hostile reception for the revised treaty (M Khadduri, op cit, p266).
45   H Batatu, op cit, p557.
46   Ibid, p563.
47   P Sluglett and M Farouk-Sluglett, op cit, p40.
48   H Batatu, op cit, p625.
49   Ibid.
50   P Sluglett and M Farouk-Sluglett, op cit, p41.
51   M Khadduri, op cit, p271.
52   Ibid, p278.
53   Ibid, p283.
54   P Sluglett and M Farouk-Sluglett, op cit, p43.
55   Ibid.
56   H Batatu, op cit, p803.
57   M S Agwani, op cit, p123.
58   P Sluglett and M Farouk-Sluglett, op cit, p52.
59   H Batatu, op cit, p849.
60   Ibid, p841.
61   U Dann, *Iraq under Qassem 1958-63* (London, 1969), pp123-124.
62   H Batatu, op cit, p834.
63   J Stork, 'The Soviet Union, the Great Powers and Iraq', in R Fernea and W Louis, (eds), *The Iraqi Revolution of 1958*: *The Old Social Classes Revisited* (London, 1991).
64   U Dann, op cit, p109.
65   M S Agwani, op cit, p118.
66   U Dann, op cit, p108.
67   P Marshall, *Intifada: Zionism, Imperialism and Palestinian Resistance* (London, 1989), p79.
68   H Batatu, op cit, p869.
69   M S Agwani, op cit, p127.
70   P Sluglett and M Farouk-Sluglett, op cit, p70.
71   M S Agwani, op cit, p130.
72   Ibid, pp138-140.
73   H Batatu, op cit, pp901-902.
74   M S Agwani, op cit, p118.
75   See Tony Cliff's *Deflected Permanent Revolution* (London, 1986) for a fuller discussion of these ideas. See also J Rees, 'The Democratic Revolution and the Socialist Revolution', *International Socialism* 83 (Summer 1999), p22.
76   P Sluglett and M Farouk-Sluglett, op cit, p47.
77   A Alexander, 'From National Liberation to Social Revolution: Egypt 1945-1953', in D Renton and K Flett (eds), *New Approaches to Socialist History* (Bristol, 2003).

78   See P Marshall, op cit, p77, for a brief account of Nasser's troubled relationship
      with the US and his turn towards the USSR and the state capitalist development
      model it offered.
79   P Marshall, op cit, p80.

Michael Kidron (1930-2003)

IAN BIRCHALL

To many readers of *International Socialism* Michael Kidron is known
only as a name that crops up in discussions of changes in capitalism after
1945. But without Kidron, who died in March, this journal would not
have developed as it did over the last 43 years.[1] He was its founding
editor and steered it through its first 20 issues from 1960 to 1965.

Kidron made many contributions to the left. Some will remember him
for helping to build Pluto Press as an independent left publisher, others
for the political atlases he produced with Ronald Segal.[2] As a theoretician
he is known for his work on the 'permanent arms economy', notably his
two books *Western Capitalism Since the War*[3] and *Capitalism and
Theory*[4] (containing key articles 'Imperialism: Highest Stage but One'
and 'International Capitalism').[5]

But Kidron was also a remarkable editor and a prolific author of
analyses and polemics. I had the enormous privilege of working with
him on the editorial board of *International Socialism* between 1963 and
1965.[6] Kidron was warm, hospitable and humorous;[7] he wrote incisively,[8]
had the capacity to draw a talented team around him, and gave encouragement and criticism to new writers. Such qualities were vital to an
editor, but they were not the essence. Kidron's supreme ability was to
use the journal as a means of developing the embryo of what was to
become the Socialist Workers Party (SWP).[9] The best tribute this journal
can pay is to recall his achievements as editor, letting him speak in his
own words.

The middle of the long post-war boom was not a quiet time for socialists. If the economic base was—temporarily—stabilised, there was a lot going on up in the superstructure. In 1956-1957 destalinisation and the crushing of the Hungarian Revolution had driven several thousand workers and intellectuals out of the Communist Party; this created a milieu in which Marxist ideas could be discussed free from Stalinist dogmatism,[10] and led to the creation, in 1960, of *New Left Review* —not just a magazine but briefly a federation of clubs at which lively and open discussion took place.[11]

Meanwhile growing opposition to the nuclear arms race led to the rise of the Campaign for Nuclear Disarmament.[12] At Easter 1960 some 100,000 people joined the march from Aldermaston. That autumn Labour Party Conference carried a resolution supporting unilateral nuclear disarmament, provoking a severe crisis when the party leader, Hugh Gaitskell,[13] refused to accept the decision.

Also in 1960 the Labour Party, seeking to cash in on the youth radicalisation produced by CND, launched the Young Socialists, which promptly became a battleground for the competing grouplets of British Trotskyism. Because most of the groups were operating with a theory 20 years out of date and sectarian habits bred of years of isolation,[14] a broad youth movement soon became a factional jungle.[15]

These times offered great opportunities to revolutionaries. *International Socialism* was conceived as a journal of analysis and debate, where rational argument might rise above sectarianism. Originally its editorial board was not limited to the Socialist Review Group, but drew from almost all the Trotskyist-derived currents except the Socialist Labour League (forerunner of the Workers Revolutionary Party). This experiment failed; by 1963 it became simply the theoretical journal of the International Socialists group. It was serious but not solemn, had glorious covers designed by Reuben Fior, and contained such delights as poems by the 28 year old Adrian Mitchell. Theoretical articles by Alasdair MacIntyre, Peter Sedgwick, Nigel Harris and above all Tony Cliff and Kidron himself provided vital support for the heated debates in the Young Socialists.

The journal also had to act as a tactical guide. When the left won at Labour Party conference, it was, paradoxically, somewhat disoriented. It fell back on legalistic reliance on the party constitution, while the right turned to the grassroots and successfully overthrew the resolution in 1961. The editorial in *International Socialism* was a model of lucidity and showed the importance of the permanent arms economy theory in establishing that the bomb was a class question; it guided IS supporters beyond possible demoralisation to a concrete strategy:

It is on defence that the left has scored its only significant victory these last years; it is on defence that the Gaitskellite Right has decided to 'fight, fight, and fight again'...

But it is...easy to exaggerate the extent of victory. However powerful the revulsion from the inhumanities of nuclear logic, it is a revulsion from one isolated component of a policy which has as yet remained unquestioned by the left at large, as by the bulk of workers. The bomb is the monster issue of a world divided into nation states, organised by power politics, a world divided—ultimately—into conflicting classes. To fight the bomb alone, as a separate issue, it might be enough to advance the 'little England' arguments given by Cousins. But to fight the complex of which the bomb is part, it is not. Gaitskell's policy has strength because it appeals to a fabric of traditions; it is 'realistic' because recognisable. The left has still to find a way to fight Gaitskell's 'internationalism' of states, with an internationalism of its own— of workers.

This is not a matter of merely finding arguments to match Gaitskell's. The right's most powerful weapon is their control of the party and trade union machine and the unscrupulous use they make of it...

The left is in no position to face Gaitskell's machine with one of its own. Our organisational resources reflect our weakness in policy magnified by the greater stress we place on convictions and on the spontaneous recruitment of people to implement them. Our strongest weapon would be to link the issue of defence with the stuff of ordinary life on which workers have shown unshakeable convictions to the point of heroism.

From this angle, it is significant that those sectors of workers that have been engaged in industrial struggle latterly—railwaymen, engineers, transport workers—are in general the most outspokenly unilateralist. It is even more significant that the central London busmen, highly critical as they are of Cousins' leadership on industrial matters, are solidly behind him on the bomb issue. It is obvious that progress for the left lies in breaking down the high stakes of nuclear diplomacy into the small chips of class struggle.

It is here that the left might show its greatest weakness. There is nothing in the record of its accepted leadership to suggest that it will organise around a programme of argument by action rather than by word, or indeed, that it sees any connection between boss and bomb. On the contrary, to date it has remained a prisoner to the basic Gaitskellite assumption: that defence is a national issue, not a class one, and has been able to find none better than the anti-unilateralist Wilson as alternative leader...

The issue of defence is too fateful for reconciliation. The left might be muddled and disorganised, but it represents a real protest at the suicidal implications of Gaitskell's policy. It represents the possibility, at least, of embedding anti-NATO politics in the soil of class struggle. It represents the unity and working class bias of the Labour Party. In order to win, the left will have to recognise at some point that the fight needs be generalised and carried beyond the arid corridors of party headquarters. Likewise, it will have to conclude that the defence problem cannot be solved in a purely British context, and that the time has come to promote—actively—internationalism as an alternative to Gaitskell's 'collective security'.[16]

A little later, when the racist right ventured onto the streets, Kidron responded in vigorous fashion:

What should the labour movement do about the fascists? Stop them physically and directly, or rely on Acts 'outlawing the dissemination of racial doctrines and practices'? One would have thought the lesson had been learnt 30 years ago and needed no repetition.

*But no, Michael Foot writing in **Tribune**'s leader column (10 August) advises against taking matters into our own hands. Forgetting the massive opposition shown the fascists recently in London, Manchester and even village Gloucestershire, ignoring the readiness of CND and Young Socialist youth for do-it-yourself politics, he writes: 'if it were accepted that the right of people to speak and demonstrate in this country should be settled by street fights and physical violence of one kind or another, the eventual casualty would be the right of free speech for many others besides the neo-Nazis. They would retaliate against left wing meetings.'*

Let them dare!

***Tribune** needs to be reminded of two basic truths. The law is **their** law, not ours—capital's not labour's... We might **use** the law sometimes, but never can we **rely** on it.*

*The second truth **Tribune** needs to ponder is that socialists are **in** this society but not **of** it. However small the socialist movement and however clogged its communications with the wider labour movement, it represents the possibility of an alternative form of society, an alternative social power. We are duty bound to assert that power where we are able.*

*If we do not, the dangers of partial fascist victories and of the roughneck politics **Tribune** fears will grow... We can't expect the constituency machine-men and parish pump tinkers to take to the streets, but **Tribune** should certainly get out of the way of ready anti-fascist fists.*[17]

In the pacifist-influenced climate of the CND milieu, this provoked protests even from within the editorial board. Subsequent history has given the verdict to Kidron.

Debate with the thinkers of the New Left was also crucial. When the *New Left Review* team produced in 1960 a collection of essays entitled *Out of Apathy*, Kidron's review was fraternal in tone, but sharp in analysis:

It would be difficult to find a better description of apathy than E P Thompson's, in his introductory essay, namely that it is the state in which people look for **private** *solutions to* **public** *evils. The essayists proceed to enlarge and refine the description... Altogether—a string of sensitive, fresh probes into the shape of apathy, but very little to do with its roots.*

We must presume that if people look for **private** *solutions to* **public** *evils they have sensed that such solutions offer some semblance of an answer to the problems they meet or are likely to meet. Surely collective action has always resulted from the demonstration of individual inadequacy when faced with certain problems? Put in this way, a discussion of apathy seems valueless without a consideration of the conditions which permit private and real solutions to be congruent to some degree, in other words the conditions which relax the imperative for collective action and allow its replacement by an aggregate of individual acts.*

What are these conditions? Collective action by whom? How do conditions and collective action react on each other? It is a weakness of the book that nowhere does it give a systematic exposition geared to these questions... If the war economy and the other factors mentioned by Thompson have anything to do with apathy, as I believe they have, it is not some wondrous alchemy that transforms them into personal withdrawal. The chaotic boom has affected different regions and different industries differently; war-sustained technical innovation has accentuated the disparity of conditions in different places of work; the anomalies of union structure and complexities of industrial structure have added their tangles, to the end that the common fate of being exploited and employed tends to be lost in the detail of being exploited in this particular manner and employed by this particular firm... It is this decline of class consciousness, this tendency towards fragmentation of the class struggle into its local constituents, which has corroded not only revolutionary socialism in this country, but also reformism and Stalinism which, in their twisted way, also owe their existence to some degree of class consciousness in the ranks of the workers. It is the filter through which capitalist prosperity must percolate to become apathy. Unfortunately, it is something whose existence does not seem to have been noticed by the authors of this volume, or if noticed, not considered sufficiently important to warrant full-length treatment.

I say 'unfortunately' in no patronising tone. The New Left has brought two very real treasures to the socialist movement: a sensitivity to the falsities and contradictions which go to make contemporary society east and west of the Iron Curtain, and a tireless assertion of human agency and **human** *(as distinct from* **class***) consciousness as the creators of history. These two characteristics are alone, eloquent protest at the indignities heaped on socialist thought by the orthodoxies of Stalinism and Social Democracy; for this alone, given the miserable scale by which we measure such things today, the New Left is a potent force for good in British socialism. But these are not enough in themselves. What is needed is an analysis of contemporary capitalism in terms of its impact on working class consciousness, prescriptions tailored to the weakness and strength of class consciousness today; in fact the* *recognition that class consciousness is the material with which we deal as socialists with a view to transforming it into a material force in its own right. Without this at its centre, socialist analysis loses its coherence and socialist programmes their reality. Both afflictions can be seen in this volume of essays... The crucial weakness of the essays is the absence of a programme. I don't mean that the essays are devoid of concrete proposals and demands... What I do mean is that each demand is put forward as a good idea in itself unrelated to material considerations of class power and consciousness, lacking in the coherence that derives from class activity and therefore unable to link up and sustain the fragments of class struggle which are always with us into a broad, integrated and thus socialist, movement. I shall take E P Thompson's concluding essay, 'Revolution', to substantiate this thesis. There is no quarrel with his rejection of the schematic, toy-soldier approach to revolution and social change held by the sectarian Left; I agree that 'it is necessary to **find out** the breaking point (in capitalism)...**in practice** by unrelenting reforming pressures in many fields, which are designed to reach a revolutionary culmination'. It is true that 'this will entail a confrontation, throughout society, between two systems, two ways of life' and that 'in this confrontation, political consciousness will become heightened'. All this is well stated, but something is missing. Confrontation between whom? One presumes, one hopes, that Thompson means labour and capital, the working class and the capitalist class (not the **idea** of progress and the **idea** of stasis), but it is nowhere clearly stated. And the tiny fuzz that surrounds this question spreads rapidly: the moment Thompson directs the working class off-stage in his social confrontation, the state of that class's political and social consciousness becomes of no immediate concern to him. It then becomes easy for Thompson to **fix** that consciousness: to **give** it its goals, to—and this is the crux—ignore the material factors in its development (just like the 'vanguardists' and 'voluntarists' which he inveighs against with such vigour). And so he blithely writes off 'disaster as the prelude to advance' forgetting that by disaster socialists have always understood those crises of capitalism—economic or political—which have fused individual and sectional struggles into classwide struggles, which have heightened consciousness of class and of the power of collective action; in other words, by disaster socialists have always understood precisely those conditions which bring together those 'unrelenting reforming pressures in many fields' at a time when they can be satisfied only through a 'revolutionary culmination'.*

*But Thompson will have none of this talk of 'conditions' and suchlike in his sweeping revolt against determinism and ends up by more or less equating the struggle for socialism with the struggle for a change of attitudes within the socialist movement: 'What is required is a new sense of immediacy'; 'a break with parliamentary fetishism'; 'research and discussion'. Yes; but how? It is time to sum up. **Out of Apathy** contains a lot of the good and a lot of the bad in the New Left. It is fresh and keenly sensitive to the more* *subtle brutalities of capitalism; it is passionate in asserting man's responsibility for history, man's creativity. But it shies away from a class analysis; it is blind to the material power of working class consciousness; it belittles the factors which impinge upon that consciousness. It has ideas, but unless these ideas become working class ideas aimed at working class power they will remain irrelevant to the socialist movement and powerless to advance it.*[18]

In the pages of *New Left Review*, Edward Thompson described *International Socialism* as 'the most constructive journal with a Trotskyist tendency in this country, most of the editorial board of which are active (and very welcome) members of the Left Club movement', but revealed some of his own confusions in responding to Kidron:

*The word 'working class' is about the most dangerous word in the rhetoric of the labour movement...the sectaries employ it platonically to indicate ideas not actually held by significant numbers of working people but ideas which they **ought** to hold, or which it would be in their **interests** to hold, if they conformed to an approved doctrinal system. In this case, a 'working class idea' is an idea of which Michael Kidron approves.*[19]

Kidron clarified the points at issue in a letter to *New Left Review*

*I see **IS** in the tradition of political **action**, a paper designed to serve the agent of social change—the working class—and therefore necessarily devoted to problems of class and class consciousness. We are not intellectual democrats—class struggle is our overriding theme. We try to study its working, to enhance it in the form of workers' independent activity. We try to link its phenomena through time and between countries. We don't think this is a narrow field. On the contrary, class relations and activity (or the absence of it) are the key to most of today's major problems; what cannot be related to them, we often find irrelevant to our aim—revolutionary social change.*

*Not so the New Left. Here is an intellectual liberalism that makes equals of all problems. True, class and class consciousness are recognised as fields of enquiry, but so is so much else, and all so well segregated. Little is done to bridge them. I defy anyone to see in the spate of words on cinema and sentiment, painting and politics the primacy of a single galvanising element, to see in fact anything but the dislocation between the **Statesman**'s back and front written large. It is not that I disagree with Thompson on class, but with its weighting in what he writes; I might agree with what the New Left as a whole thinks of the matter, but I suspect that it hardly gives it a thought.*

*In a word, to my mind **IS** is geared to action; **NLR** is not. Action demands priorities of preoccupation; inaction can do without.*[20]

But the most important debate was between reform and revolution. To be a revolutionary at all in the early 1960s was far from easy; to argue the case for revolution without relying on outdated language and outdated analyses required real intellectual clarity. *International Socialism* carried a major debate on left reformism, initiated by the labour historian Henry Collins. Kidron's contribution extended far beyond the technicalities of the permanent arms economy to lay the basis for a political strategy. He began by showing the fundamental instability of modern capitalism:

> *For reformists capitalist instability is subject to cure within the system; for revolutionary socialists it is not. The reformist will point to the absence of major slumps since before the war; the revolutionary—apart from a lunatic fringe who see in every visit to the labour exchange a prelude to hunger marches—will accept the fact but question its relevance. Slumps have never defined the system; they merely indicated, viciously and publicly, its contradictory nature. Ultimately they derive from factors which are as inherent in capitalism today as they ever were, and which remain as powerful a source of instability.*
>
> *Were it not that the productive forces of society are controlled by an infinitesimal minority of its members, the capitalists, the disposition of its resources over and above what is required for renewal would present no problem. It would conform to a pattern formulated by all in terms of present and projected needs and wishes. Were it not for competition amongst capitalists, whether organised in monopolies or not, there would be no compulsion for them to accumulate these surpluses and reinvest them in a constant, unplanned expansion of the productive structure. These statements are axiomatic in my argument. Without both these factors there would be no reason for the blind accumulations of capital—blind in the sense that it bears no immediate relation to the consumer needs of society—that has always defined the capitalist system. And it is this compulsive accumulation, the expansion of capacity in response to the exigencies of competition rather than to the needs of society, that has been the final cause of the periodic crises of overproduction that punctuated the development of capitalism until quite recently. It is also for Marx the underlying factor in the long-term decline in the rate of profit which, by lowering the ceiling of booms and shortening their duration, presaged for him a future of increasingly catastrophic slumps.*[21]

He went on to show the implications for class consciousness and political intervention:

> *An obvious outcome is the decline of reformism as a political movement. Whether it is measured in the shrinking individual membership of the Labour Party, or in the changing nature of the party as Gaitskell drags it towards*

Brandt's SDP, or in the utter confusion of the honest reformist left around **Tribune***, the symptoms of decline are all too apparent. On balance workers still vote Labour—although the balance among young workers is slowly tilting away—but the expectation of improvement from changes at Westminster is dying, and with it the degree of political involvement on the part of the working class.*

This is not to say that workers are any less interested in reforms than they have ever been. The permanent arms economy has provided full employment; it has created the expectation of continued full employment and to that extent a degree of self confidence and indifference to authority little known in working class history. It is hardly to be expected that this confidence and bargaining power will be wasted. On the contrary, far from there being less interest in reforms and less involvement in gaining them, there are more; what has happened is a change in the forms and arena of struggle and, to an even more marked extent, a change in the troops.

In a word, workers have become their own reformists. Where before they pursued their reformist aims—minimum wages, maximum hours, health and other welfare services—by sending **representatives** *to parliament, now, with the decanting of power out of parliament into the huge private complexes that control the economy, they take steps to achieve the same end directly,* **without intermediaries** *other than shop stewards' or similar local organisations.*

It is no part of this argument to idolise this development after the manner of the syndicalists. It has unpleasant aspects. However militant a body of workers, or successful in improving their own conditions, unless their militancy is generalised into political action, it can only result in deepening the gulf between themselves and less fortunate sections, those that are either too old or not lucky enough to work in the concentrated and growing industries. The pattern of capitalist success merely assumes a cloth cap. Their activity is sectional, it multiplies the fragmentation of their class, substitutes a local, ad hoc consciousness for class consciousness, leads to a distrust of political ideas and political organisations. The indictment is long and could be extended. Nevertheless, these things are happening. To deny it, or the relevance of sectional militancy or do it yourself reformism to modern conditions is to ignore contemporary capitalism's most characteristic features and the realism of the working class response to them.

But if there is no case for idolatry, there is equally no cause for despair. By becoming his own reformist the worker rejects the inhibiting influence of the organised reformist party. It is he, directly involved in his local primary organisation, who bears the brunt of the conflict with capital; it is he who takes the decision, with scant reference to authority, to act; and it is his appreciation of the relation of forces between those fragments of capital and labour with which he has direct experience that informs his activity. For him reform and revolution are not separate activities, enshrined in distinct and separate organisational loyalties; his transition from reform to revolution is natural, immediate and unhampered by the vested interests of a reformist organisation and one eminently responsive to changing circumstances.

It is here that the discussion of capitalist stability ties in with the argument. Were the system as stable as Collins suggests, there would be no question of transition. It is only because of its fundamentally crisis-ridden nature that we can posit the transformation of sectional consciousness and loyalties into their class equivalents, and therewith a change of society, sharp and cataclysmic, as a realistic alternative to the deadly status quo.

To say this is not to underestimate the difficulties of transition. Reality is infinitely more complex and contradictory than appears here. And working class history is a confusion of revolutionary opportunities lost, of revolutionary consciousness castrated by the very fragmentation that has enabled sections of the class to attain a high order of self mobilisation. But this is where we must stop. To continue would entail a detailed discussion of the role of a revolutionary party, the problems of its formation and the forms it could take.

After 1968, for reasons that were probably partly personal and partly political, Kidron's role in the organisation became much less central. But if it was Tony Cliff's relentless determination that enabled the SWP to become what it is today, Mike Kidron's part in educating the generation that seized the opportunities of 1968 and after should never be forgotten.

Notes

1   The first *International Socialism* (containing an article by Kidron on recent strikes) appeared in 1958. This was a one-off and a new series (quarterly, and from 1973 monthly) was launched at Easter 1960. This lasted till issue 104 in 1978. The new series, now approaching its 100th number, began in 1978.

2   For an overview of Kidron's life see Richard Kuper's obituary in *The Guardian*, 27 March 2003, Chris Harman, 'Permanent Legacy', *Socialist Review*, April 2003, or my own piece in *Revolutionary History* vol 8, no 3 (2003).

3   M Kidron, *Western Capitalism Since the War* (London, 1968); revised Penguin edition (Harmondsworth,1970).

4   M Kidron, *Capitalism and Theory* (London, 1974).

5   For a critique of Kidron's economic work see C Harman, 'Better a Valid Insight than a Wrong Theory', *International Socialism* 1:100 (July 1977); C Harman, *Explaining the Crisis* (London, 1984); and Harman's article 'Analysing Imperialism' in this issue of the journal.

6   I owed my position to my knowledge of foreign languages, and not to my (negligible) political experience.

7   One of the joys of joining the International Socialists was to discover that one was allowed to have a sense of humour. For much of the Trotskyist left jokes were frowned on, unless they were recycled bits of abuse from Trotsky's less well judged polemics. But while Tony Cliff never told a joke that did not have a direct political message, Kidron's humour was more playful and self ironic, a recognition that however good the analysis there was always something left over.

8   He characteristically used a condensed and abbreviated style that often suggested he was submitting his copy by telegram at a pound a word. His work often had to be reread carefully to get the full wealth of meaning.

9   In 1960 the Socialist Review Group had less than 50 members; it changed its name to the International Socialists in 1962 and by 1965 had grown to over 200.

10   For a sense of the period read the earlier sections of D Widgery, *The Left in Britain* (Harmondsworth, 1976).

11   See I Birchall, 'The Autonomy of Theory: A Short History of *New Left Review*', *International Socialism* 2:10 (Autumn 1980).

12   For a history of CND see R Bulkeley et al, '"If at first you don't succeed": fighting against the bomb in the 1950s and 1960s', *International Socialism* 2:11 (Winter 1980).

13   At this time Labour leaders were elected by the parliamentary party alone.

14   For the crisis of post-1945 Trotskyism see T Cliff, *A World to Win* (London, 2000), and S Bornstein and A Richardson, *War and the International* (London, 1986).

15   To get a sense of the atmosphere in the Young Socialists read 'A Weekend with the Lumpentrots', *Young Guard* (June 1964), describing the factional degeneration of a YS weekend school. This appeared under the name Mike Caffoor but was written by Jim Higgins. Jim died last year and a collection of his political writings is currently in preparation.

16   'Labour and the Bomb', *International Socialism* 1:3 (Winter 1960). This was before I joined the editorial board, and I cannot be sure it came from Kidron's pen. Style and intellectual rigour suggest it did; if someone else drafted it, they were heavily influenced by Kidron.

17   'Fists Against Fascists', *International Socialism* 1:10 (Autumn 1962).

18   'Two Left Feet', *International Socialism* 1:2 (Autumn 1960).

19   'Revolution Again!', *New Left Review* 1:6 (November/December 1961).

20   'Intellectual Liberalism?', *New Left Review* 1:7 (January/February 1961).

21   'Rejoinder to Left Reformism', *International Socialism* 1:7 (Winter 1961).

The revolt in Parma[1]

GUIDO PICELLI

*In August 1922, just ten weeks before Mussolini seized power, one of the biggest ever confrontations in history took place between fascists and anti-fascists. Led by a Socialist Party MP, Guido Picelli, the local branch of the **Arditi del popolo** (People's Shock Troops), a national anti-fascist organisation created in June 1921, had managed to bring together the many different strands of the Italian left.*

For six days 20,000 armed blackshirts threw themselves against the working class of the central Italian town of Parma. This was the only city which had so far held out against fascist attacks, primarily due to strong local traditions of unity.

For a long time Parma was one of the main centres of Italian syndicalism. The local trades council had as its leader some of the most 'apolitical' leaders of the period: Michele Bianchi, Filippo Corridoni and Alceste De Ambris. Apart from a few towns in the lower Parma area, over many years of struggle the Socialist Party had neither managed to extend their influence throughout the area, nor to break workers and peasants from the anarchoid propaganda of syndicalist leaders.

The situation changed only after the Great War. Following the betrayal of those who had supported intervention, the majority of the Parma working class joined the official trades council and moved towards the Socialist Party. The syndicalists, who were by now divided into two factions (pro-war interventionists and the anarchist USI), only had a small number of organised workers behind them. Immediately after the Livorno congress of January 1921,[2] a significant number of workers and peasants joined the Communist Party. A small number of peasants in the upper Parma area joined the Catholic Popular Party, which in Parma had a major leader in Giuseppe Micheli, then minister of agriculture.

These divisions did not reflect the will of the masses, who always had a strong sense of unity. They had been artificially created and maintained by social democratic leaders and old syndicalist activists, who looked upon unity as the end of their policy of alliances with open and sworn enemies of the working class. Their efforts to sabotage all attempts from below to create a single working class organisation were such that Amilcare De Ambris (secretary of the syndicalist trades council and currently a fascist) and Alberto Simonini (reformist socialist secretary of the official trades council) were sometimes beaten up by organised workers.

Parma has a population of about 70,000 and is divided in two by the river of the same name: the largest half is called 'new Parma' and is inhabited mainly by the bourgeoisie, while the other half, 'old Parma', or *Oltretorrente*, has a largely working class population.

The working class of Parma has a history of erecting barricades which goes back to the 1898 revolt and perhaps even further. The agricultural strike of 1908, which lasted for months throughout the province, was one of the most important peasant struggles in Italy.

The economic structure of the province of Parma is made up of large, small and medium landholdings, with tied tenants, sharecroppers and day labourers. The city and its suburbs are characterised by artisan workshops and light industry—engineering works, shoe factories, perfumes, sugar, pasta factories and preserves.

Locally fascism never managed, either through propaganda or agitation, to develop and dominate as it has done in other areas. The *Arditi del popolo*, which had arisen in 1921 due to the initiative of workers from different political backgrounds, in opposition to the wishes of many of the leaders of political and trade union organisations, managed to keep the blackshirts in check for over a year, both in the city and the countryside, through an incessant array of defensive and offensive action.

This movement differed slightly in Parma compared to other areas due to its greater discipline and its technical application of the tactics of armed street fighting. The command structure of the *Arditi del popolo* had foreseen a huge 'punitive expedition' a long time beforehand, and apart from preparing people mentally, also developed a defensive plan and obtained the necessary means to face and repel the enemy. Squad leaders were selected from workers with military experience, and had the task of training other men, while those charged with special services were called upon to keep in contact with soldiers stationed in Parma in order to obtain weapons and ammunition.

The Labour Alliance, created due to the pressure of the masses, called a 'legalitarian' national general strike for 31 July 1922. But the central committee of the alliance, under the influence of social democrat leaders, called it off and ordered people back to work as soon as Mussolini threatened reprisals.[3] Events then moved very quickly. Overall the *Arditi del popolo*, without a party which mapped out a political line and revolutionary objectives to be reached, had exhausted its offensive potential in straightforward counter-attacks against the fascists. In Emilia, Veneto, Liguria and Tuscany, where working class resistance had been greatest, a vacuum had been created among workers due to numerous losses. Linking defensive actions became difficult and areas were repeatedly terrorised by the enemy's armed gangs; the masses were frequently forced to retreat. But fascism's victory was not yet complete. There was still one place in Emilia that was resisting—Parma.

The first contingents of blackshirts arrived on the night of 1-2 August, in lorries which had come from all over Emilia, Veneto, Tuscany and the Marches. They were armed with brand new rifles, pistols and hand grenades, together with a huge amount of ammunition. They were experienced fighters, tried and tested in the tactics of 'punitive expeditions'.

They assembled around the station, and the following consuls were at the head of the columns: Arrivabene, Barbiellini, Farinacci, Moschini, Ponzi and Ranieri. The commander-in-chief of the expedition, which quickly rose to a total of 20,000 men, was Italo Balbo.[4] Signorile, the police chief of Parma, after having told the local committee of the Labour Alliance that he could do nothing to stop the blackshirts assembling, withdrew his men from the two police stations in the *Oltretorrente* area, thus giving them a free hand.

As soon as the news spread of the fascists' arrival, the local leadership of the *Arditi del popolo* immediately called a meeting with squad leaders and gave them instructions to build barricades, trenches and barbed wire defences using any material available. At dawn, when the order was given to get the guns out and launch the insurrection, working class people took to the streets—as bold as the waters of a river bursting its banks. With their shovels, pickaxes, iron bars, and all sorts of tools, they helped the *Arditi del popolo* dig up the cobblestones and tram tracks, digging trenches, erecting barricades using carts, benches, timber, iron girders and anything else they could get their hands on. Men and women, old people and young people from all parties and from no party were all there, united in a single iron will—resist and fight.

In just a few hours the working class areas of the city started to look like a major battle zone. This area was divided into four sectors: *Nino Bixio* and *Massimo D'Azeglio* in *Oltretorrente*; *Naviglio* and *Aurelio Saffi* in 'new

Parma'. The number of squads in each sector was in direct proportion to its size: 22 in *Oltretorrente* as a whole, six in *Naviglio* and four in *Aurelio Saffi*. Each squad was made up of eight to ten men, and their weaponry was made up of model 1891 rifles, muskets, army pistols, automatic revolvers and SIPE hand grenades. Only half of these men had a rifle or musket. All the entrances to squares, roads and alleyways were blocked by defensive structures, and at spots viewed as being tactically important, positions were reinforced by barbed wire and mines were laid. Church towers were transformed into numbered watchtowers. Throughout these fortified zones power passed into the hands of the *Arditi del popolo* command, which was made up of a small number of workers which had been elected by the squads earlier. These workers were allocated various responsibilities: defence and organisation, provision of food, and first aid. Shop owners and the middle class sympathised with the rebels, and provided them with food and a variety of other goods.

The fascists opened fire just before 9am. Attacks and counter-attacks continued along the front line throughout the day, without producing any substantial changes in the situation. During the night there was some shooting and minor sorties by enemy detachments, which were identified in the *Naviglio* through the use of flares.

The following morning Balbo attacked at the head of a detachment of blackshirts from *piazzale della Pilota*. Crossing Verdi Bridge they attempted to break through the lines of the *Arditi del popolo*. But as soon as they caught sight of the first barricades they understood the very grave danger they would have faced if they took another step, so they gave up and retreated. Immediately afterwards the fascists opened fire again from the right side of the river; and from open positions tested our lines with angry fusillades in an attempt to break through. But the defenders of the 'workers' citadel', laying on the ground on the left bank and always under some kind of cover, calmly returned fire and took careful aim— frequently managing to hit a very visible enemy.

Simultaneously, in 'new Parma' offices of professionals who were known to be socialists were ransacked. But the fiercest attacks took place against the *Naviglio* area which, due to its shape, was the most difficult to defend. After several hours of fighting this entire sector was almost surrounded—blackshirts advanced in tight formations from *via Venti Settembre*, determined to score a decisive victory. At that crucial moment only one response was possible—come out and counter-attack. Indeed the *Arditi del popolo* leapt up from their positions singing *Bandiera Rossa*, and ran towards the enemy. They were heavily outnumbered and one of them, Giuseppe Mussini, a worker, fell dead. But they didn't stop. Their singing grew louder and the bullets flew from the rifles which were burning in their hands. The fascists were shocked to see this handful of heroes, and imagined that there were who knows how many fighters and weapons waiting behind the barricades, in the trenches and inside houses, so they fell back even beyond *Barriera Garibaldi*.

On the third day things worsened again in the *Naviglio* area. The fascists blocked all routes through to *Oltretorrente*, all links were severed. All homing pigeons were quickly used up. Finally, after a lot of difficulty, a female worker managed to get through to the *Arditi del popolo* command in 'old Parma' and deliver a message she had hidden in her hair:

> *Two more deaths: Ugo Avanzini and Nino Gazzola. Our dispatch rider has been wounded. There is no food, and ammunition is almost exhausted. We urgently need bullets for rifles and revolvers, otherwise we will be forced to retreat to* **Oltretorrente** *tonight. We await orders: Sector commander.*

The woman returned with as much ammunition as she could carry hidden in her clothes, along with the following reply: 'Our orders are to hold your ground even if it means dying. We have faith in you. We'll find a way of gettting you food and ammunition as soon as possible: Workers' defence command.'

We needed to deny our adversary even the smallest of victories, given that the first symptoms of demoralisation were beginning to show. Orders were obeyed to the letter and we kept our positions. Later on communication was re-established with *Naviglio*, which received ammunition and wheat taken from the local windmill. Operations also began to improve in the *Oltretorrente*—the requisition and distribution of food, first aid points, field kitchens, patrols, the relaying of information, and the reinforcement of defensive positions. Women took a very active part in all of this, turning up everywhere to lend a hand and to give encouragement.

In the meantime the authorities had handed power over to the army, which contacted the local committee of the Labour Alliance, ie leaders of the Socialist Party and pro-war and official trade unionists. As these individuals had been unable to openly block the masses' decision to go to the barricades, so as not to be exposed for what they were, they felt they had been deprived of authority and placed into the background, and therefore agreed to negotiate a compromise, committing themselves to persuade workers to stop their resistance. A socialist lawyer named Pancrazi and police commissioner Di Sero were the link between these individuals and the army commander, General Lodomez.

The outcome of all this manoeuvring emerged on day five when the army, believing that Socialist Party and trade union leaders represented the masses, or at least were able to influence them, sent a battalion of soldiers into *Oltretorrente* to dismantle the barricades and trenches, and told people that the fascists would withdraw if people disarmed. But here they found a different kind of authority, effectively that of the masses, in the shape of the *Arditi del popolo* command. Nobody had thought it necessary to speak to them but they couldn't be ignored.

Here was their reply: 'The trenches mustn't be touched, as they are a legitimate means of defence for workers and their communities against 20,000 blackshirts who have come here from all quarters.'

The officers protested, saying that they had their orders, but workers didn't back down—they had their orders as well! The mood of the soldiers was such that it dissuaded the officers from making a big fuss. After two hours the battalion was withdrawn. Attempts at a compromise had failed, as did this attempt to disarm the workers.

In the early hours of day six we were informed from reliable sources that the fascist leadership had decided to launch a major attack against *Oltretorrente* at 3pm. Although we were unable to discover their plans in detail, in any event the command believed that the enemy would focus their efforts on a breach to the left of our lines. It was here that we faced the greatest risk of being outflanked—through the park which runs along the built-up area of *Oltretorrente*, which could be accessed from the ring-road to the north of the city.

One of the general rules of war, and therefore of street fighting, is to never leave the initiative to your enemy. And in a situation in which you discover their intentions and the plan of attack, you must foil them by attacking earlier, forcing them to change their entire strategy through a determined and unexpected action.

Unfortunately we were not able to take the offensive as we did not have enough rifles and ammunition, which had been severely depleted over three days of resistance. It was impossible to get any last minute help from the surrounding countryside, as the fascists had sent patrols into the most notorious areas in order to stop any link-ups with the city.

However, a massive defence plan was agreed using anything available, which would have involved every one of the enemy in all kinds of fighting to the end. After having called a meeting of the squad leaders, the *Arditi del popolo* command made a rapid inspection of the entire area. The morale of the masses was very high—it almost seemed as if the news of the blackshirts' imminent attack had fuelled courage and enthusiasm even further. In armed combat, one of the most important elements of success is belief in victory. And it was interesting to observe that everybody had an absolute 'belief'—no one had the slightest doubt. Bombs were prepared in houses, along with clubs studded with razor blades, knives and nails, as well as acid bombs. A 17 year old girl waved an axe from the windows of her hovel and shouted out to her comrades in the street, 'If they come I'm ready for them!' Containers full of petrol were distributed to women because, according to our defence plan, if fascists managed to get into *Oltretorrente*, fighting would then take place on a house by house, alleyway by alleyway, street by street basis. No quarter would be shown—inflammable material would be thrown at the fascists, and our positions would be burned and totally destroyed.

The *Arditi del popolo* squads were divided into groups of three or four men and deployed in the following fashion: ten along the river bank covering Caprazuzza, Mezzo and Verdi bridges; twelve along the northern flank—stationed on roofs and attics so as to be able to fire on the park. Every worker who had either a firearm or any kind of offensive weapon was deployed in groups at various points, ready to run to where they were needed. Our lookouts followed all the enemy's movements very carefully.

The first shots rang out at about 2pm, on the right hand side of the river, and were aimed at *Nino Bixio* with enfilades at two other areas. A few hours earlier Ulisse Corazza, an artisan and Popular Party councillor (the Catholic party), had presented himself to a squad leader with his own musket, and asked to take part in the fighting alongside the *Arditi del popolo*. He suffered a serious head wound from a rifle shot, and died a few minutes later. However all of this was intended to deceive the defenders as to the real goals of their plan of attack, as detachments of blackshirts had simultaneously moved on the left of *Oltretorrente* and had advanced into the park, heading for the city wall. This wasn't a surprise, as the *Arditi del popolo* had expected such a move. So fusillades immediately rang out as planned, thus causing the enemy the greatest number of losses possible with the minimum use of ammunition. Although their pressure and aggression were initially very strong, little by little they weakened and a few hours later ceased altogether. The exhortations of their commanders made no difference—it was impossible to advance under the fire of working class snipers. Slowly, using bushes for cover, the blackshirts fell back to their original positions. During the night the fascists limited themselves to a few nuisance shots which had no effect at all.

On the morning of 7 August our observers noticed columns moving from one point of the outskirts to another in a confused and disordered fashion. This was something new; but it wasn't possible to immediately understand what was about to happen. The following information reached *Oltretorrente*: 'The blackshirts are very unhappy about their losses. Orders given by their leaders are not always obeyed. Panic is spreading.' This disorder began to increase steadily, until it became generalised. The fascists, who were by this stage no longer in military formation, were roaming about in all directions in a great rush—with no command structure—jumping onto trains that were leaving, onto lorries, bicycles, or going on foot. This wasn't a retreat, but the scattering of large groups of men who clambered aboard any means of transport they found, or who ran through the streets, or into the countryside, as if they were frightened of being chased.

Once the news of the fascists' departure spread, the working class population on both sides of the river rushed into the streets, some carrying weapons, and improvised huge marches in an indescribable explosion of enthusiasm—red flags were hung from the windows in 'old Parma'. The news of the working class's victory spread rapidly in the surrounding area, where terrified local landowners abandoned their houses and ran away towards Cremona, as they had heard that the *Arditi del popolo* were coming.

The military authorities were worried; they were concerned that as a result of the blackshirts' defeat the movement could spread out from the city to surrounding areas. This was exactly what the *Arditi del popolo* command intended, and at that very moment messengers were sent out with an appeal to the working class organisations of Milan and La Spezia. Therefore a state of siege was proclaimed—and the dismantling of trenches and barricades was ordered to be finished by 3pm. The command considered the new situation which the authorities had created, and realised it was materially impossible to stop the army—made up of two local infantry regiments with machine gun and armoured detachments, together with a cavalry regiment and considerable artillery—from gaining control of *Oltretorrente*, *Naviglio* and *Aurelio Saffi*.

At 3.10pm Colonel Simondetti, after firing a blank from one of the two cannons on Mezzo Bridge, advanced with armoured cars, machine guns and soldiers, occupying all the working class areas and ordering his troops to clear the streets.

Balbo's forces had disintegrated—they were nowhere to be seen. On the fifth day a large-scale 'punitive expedition' against the working class of Parma had become a disaster. The blackshirts suffered 39 dead and 150 wounded, while the defenders suffered five dead and several wounded.

Two and a half months later, shortly before the March on Rome, the fascists again discussed the situation in Parma. In his book *Diario 1922*, published two years ago [1932], Balbo spoke of a meeting which took place in Rome with Mussolini, and of another of the whole Fascist Party leadership:

> One of the issues we still need to settle is Parma. This is the last stronghold of anti-national forces, and acts as both a sanctuary and as moral support for Italian subversion. Mussolini agrees with the plan of action I outlined to him… Any action against Parma must precede any move towards an insurrection.

Fascist leaders believed that mobilisation for the March on Rome could have encountered some serious difficulties if working class resistance in a strategic point of Emilia Romagna had not been liquidated beforehand. Yet no second attack against Parma was ever attempted. New developments led to sudden changes—fascism, heavy industry and the monarchy had come to an agreement over the so called March on Rome.[5]

With hindsight, one can make the following points as regards the events recounted above:

(1) Until this point political and military problems and the theory of civil war had either been undervalued or even totally ignored; yet today we are obliged to treat it as an absolute necessity.

(2) As regards the outcome of this armed revolt, the Italian working class experienced an enormous success with the revolt in Parma—urban fighting won in conditions of great numerical and military inferiority.

(3) Even if the *Arditi del popolo* had managed to pull the mass of working class people into armed resistance, what was lacking was the preparatory work among soldiers who, given their mood and specific situation, could have been persuaded to show active solidarity with the proletariat. Similarly insufficient and negative were linkages with the surrounding provinces, which broke down in the most difficult moments of the struggle: a co-ordinated peasant movement would have enabled us to have immediately launched an offensive.

(4) The local trade union and social democratic leaders were completely unmasked. Through the use of demagogic language, they hid their real objective of following the needs of the bourgeoisie. While they hypocritically talked about anti-fascism and the masses' interests, in practice they were betraying these interests by blocking and hampering the spontaneous formation of a united front from below—thus playing into the hands of the fascists. Apart from our technical preparations, the reason behind our success was above all the fact that the working class of Parma had been able to free itself and place its false leaders—the 'enemy within' the working class—to one side, thus confronting fascism with its own strongly united forces.

(5) Our party, which was then affected by extremism, failed to understand the nature of the *Arditi del popolo* and tried to stop our members from individually joining their ranks. In that period the masses were either part of the *Arditi del popolo* or were their sympathisers. The theories of Bordiga,[6] a typical example of a petty bourgeois mentality, had led the party into opportunism and isolation. Through individual communist participation in the *Arditi del popolo* squads, the party would have been able to influence the whole organisation and to have won the leadership. With detailed preparatory work and membership of reformist trade unions and the army, the party would have been able to direct the movement towards a series of precise objectives, pulling the rest of the masses towards armed insurrection through the *Arditi del popolo*, stopping the growth of reaction in Italy and changing the course of history.

Notes

    Translated and annotated by Tom Behan.

1   Originally published in *Lo Stato Operaio* (*Workers' State*), October 1934, an Italian Communist Party journal published in exile in Paris. Picelli joined the Communist Party in 1923, and later served five years in fascist jails before emigrating. He died in 1937, fighting in the Spanish Civil War.

2   The founding congress of the Italian Communist Party was held in the Tuscan port of Livorno in January 1921.

3   This strike, called in 'defence of political and trade union freedoms', was prepared in a hurried and half-hearted fashion. Apart from Parma, it was a disaster for the left, leading to another wave of fascist attacks.

4   Balbo was probably the main organiser of fascist 'punitive expeditions' in central Italy, and later became a minister in Mussolini's government.

5   Picelli is referring to the ruling class's decision to make Mussolini prime minister, which the fascists celebrated in their 'March on Rome' at the end of October 1922.

6   Amadeo Bordiga (1889-1970) was leader of the Communist Party from 1921 to 1924, and was expelled in 1930. He took a hostile attitude to the *Arditi del popolo*, and argued for much smaller and ineffective military squads—made up only of party members.

The legacy of Christopher Hill

BRIAN MANNING

Christopher Hill was especially conscious of the interaction between past and present. Attitudes towards the past and interpretations of history alter as a result of changes in contemporary society.[1] For him the most dramatic and far-reaching examples of the revolutionising of historical studies by present day politics were 'women's history' and 'history from below'.

'Women's history, I suppose, is the best advertisement for the beneficial result of asking of the past questions which arise from the present... One of the things I am most ashamed of is that for decades I...somehow assumed that' political demands being made only in the name of men 'had to be taken for granted in 17th century England. But if we are to understand that society we have to ask why it was taken for granted... Once we ask the question, other questions are opened up' and there has to be a huge rethinking about the past.[2]

'The most fruitful change in historical attitudes in my time', he wrote, 'I think has been the emergence of "history from below"—the realisation that ordinary people have a history, that they may have played a greater part in determining the shape of the historical process, whether for change or for continuity, than we have thought'.[3] Attention had to shift from nobles, gentry, merchants and clergy to peasants, artisans and 'the poor', and their significant roles in the English Revolution. This was the product of a growing sense in the present that 'ordinary people' (I dislike the term) can change the world, and take inspiration from the history of popular movements.

Christopher Hill was opposed to the 'departmentalisation of history' and chopping it up into bits labelled 'constitutional history', 'political history', 'economic history', 'religious history', 'literary history', 'women's history', and 'people's history'.[4]

> *The historian should not stay on the surface of events; his or her interest should not be limited to State Papers, Acts and Ordinances, decisions of judges and local magistrates... He or she should listen—carefully and critically—to ballads, plays, pamphlets, newspapers, tracts...to every source that can help him or her to get the feel of how people lived and in what ways their sensitivity differed from ours... The historian must listen to alchemists and astrologers no less than to bishops, to demands of London crowds; and he or she must try to understand the motivation of rioters, whether they are labelled anti-Catholic or anti-enclosure rioters or simply food rioters.[5]*

Whatever his starting point, Hill's stress was always on the interconnectedness of different aspects of history, whether religion and society, or literature and politics.[6] This may be regarded as a chief aim of the Marxist interpretation of history. In his economic history of early modern England he said, 'My aim has been all through to emphasise interaction between politics and economics, seeing neither as a sufficient cause in itself.' Political revolution has economic causes, and political revolution transforms social and economic life.[7]

In the 1930s and 1940s he thought that the pendulum of historical studies had swung too far towards economic interpretations and he set himself to revive 'interest in the ideas that motivated the 17th century revolutionaries'.[8] He recognised that the English Revolution took place in a world very different from our own —a world dominated by religion and religious idioms. He sought to dissociate Marxist history from economic determinism, and condemned the 'crude' belief that 'the material conflicts are the only ones deserving serious analysis'.[9] 'Marx himself did not fall into the error of thinking that men's ideas were merely a pale reflection of economic needs...'[10] 'Any adequate interpretation of the English Revolution must give full place to questions of religion and church government, must help us to grasp the political and social implications of theological heresy'.[11]

He devoted a great deal of his historical work to the history of ideas. In his view this was essential for the study of revolution: 'Men...do not break lightly with the past: if they are to challenge conventionally accepted standards they must have an alternative body of ideas to support them... Almost by definition, a great revolution cannot take place without ideas'.[12] 'Shifts in ideas are therefore necessary if a revolution is to take place'.[13] This is as relevant to present day as to past politics.

'What mattered in the English Revolution', wrote Hill, 'was that the ruling class was deeply divided at a time when there was much combustible material among the lower classes usually excluded from politics'.[14] The ruling class was split over constitutional and ecclesiastical matters, but some artisans, apprentices and women demanded voices in questions of church and state. Hill suggested that there were two revolutions in mid-17th century England: one was a struggle for power between two sections of the ruling class, and the other was a struggle for a share in power by plebeian elements, often linked with demands for reform of the legal system and for the abolition of tithes (taxes for payment of the clergy), and sometimes expressing hostility to the ruling class. The latter frightened the propertied classes to reunite in order to reassert their dominance and settled the final outcome of the revolutions.[15]

Hill's preliminary interpretation of the English Revolution was put forward in 1940,[16] and elaborated in a volume of documents, edited with Edmund Dell (a future Labour minister) in 1949, in which the introduction declared:

> *Our subject here is the story of how one social class was driven from power by another, and how the form of state power appropriate to the needs of the first was replaced by one appropriate to those of the second. The first class, the ruling class in England in the first decades of the 17th century, was a semi-feudal landed aristocracy... The new class which grew up inside English feudal society...was the bourgeoisie—merchants, industrialists, and landowners regarding their estates primarily as a source of money profits rather than as a means of maintaining feudal followers.*[17]

Intensive research into the parties of the civil war rendered this interpretation unsustainable, and the struggle could not be demonstrated as having been between a 'bourgeoisie' and a 'semi-feudal landed aristocracy'. In the 1960s and 1970s Hill abandoned the bourgeoisie.

'The Marxist conception of a bourgeois revolution, which I find the most helpful model for understanding the English Revolution,' he wrote, 'does not mean a revolution made by the bourgeoisie'.[18] There was no self conscious bourgeoisie which planned and willed the revolution. But the English Revolution was a bourgeois revolution because its outcome, though glimpsed by few of its participants, 'was the establishment of conditions far more favourable to the development of capitalism than those which prevailed before 1640'.[19]

In the conjuncture of upheavals in the 1640s and 1650s, social forces and ideas were juxtaposed to each other, sometimes unrelated to the development of capitalism, sometimes assimilating with the development of capitalism. This conjuncture included 'not only the

individualism of those who wished to make money by doing what they
wanted with their own, but also the individualism of those who wished to
follow their own consciences in worshipping god, and whose consciences led them to challenge the institutions of a stratified hierarchical
society'.[20] Among the outcomes stressed by Hill was the overthrow by
popular resistance of the monopoly of the state church, to which all sub-
jects were obliged by law to belong, and the creation of space for people
to have alternatives and choices in religion, in what has been described
as 'free market Christianity'. The expropriation of poor peasants was not
prevented by popular resistance during the revolution, and the process
continued by which more and more people became landless and dependent on working as wage labourers. During the revolution black slave
labour was imposed in British colonies, the slave trade was established,
and white supremacy was asserted. This was confirmed and extended
after 1660. Hill argued powerfully that the outcome of the revolution
facilitated the development of capitalism. This was not the objective of
the revolution but the result of social forces drawn in the wake of the
revolution.[21]

Notes

1   C Hill, *Change and Continuity in 17th Century England* (London, 1974), p284.
2   C Hill, 'History and the Present', in *A Nation of Change and Novelty* (London,
      1990), pp245-246.
3   Ibid, p245.
4   C Hill, *Intellectual Origins of the English Revolution* (Oxford, 1965), p300.
5   C Hill, *The English Bible and the Seventeenth Century Revolution* (London,
      1993), pp436-437.
6   C Hill, *Milton and the English Revolution* (London, 1977).
7   C Hill, *Reformation to Industrial Revolution 1530-1780* (London, 1969), p14.
8   C Hill, *Intellectual Origins of the English Revolution*, op cit, p6.
9   C Hill, *Economic Problems of the Church* (Oxford, 1956), ppx, xiii-xiv.
10   C Hill, *Intellectual Origins of the English Revolution*, op cit, p3.
11   C Hill, *Puritanism and Revolution* (London, 1958), p29.
12   C Hill, *Intellectual Origins of the English Revolution*, op cit, pp1, 5-6.
13   C Hill, *Change and Continuity in 17th Century England*, op cit, p282.
14   C Hill, 'A Bourgeois Revolution?', in J G A Pocock (ed), *Three British Revolutions:
      1641, 1688, 1776* (Princeton, 1980), p124.
15   C Hill, *The Century of Revolution 1603-1714* (Edinburgh, 1961), p188; C Hill,
      The World Turned Upside Down (London, 1972), p12.
16   C Hill, *The English Revolution, 1640* (London, 1940).
17   C Hill and E Dell (eds), *The Good Old Cause: The English Revolution of 1640-60*
      (London, 1949), pp20-21.
18   C Hill, *Change and Continuity in 17th Century England*, op cit, pp279-280.
19   C Hill, 'A Bourgeois Revolution?', op cit, pp110, 111, 115, 134.
20   Ibid, p112.
21   Ibid; C Hill, 'The Place of the 17th Century Revolution in English History', in *A
      Nation of Change and Novelty*, op cit.

Réseau européen de revues marxistes critiques

A European network of critical Marxist journals

Le Projet K sera présent à Lausanne dans le cadre des rencontres des 15 & 16 mai contre le sommet du G8. Il proposera trois tables rondes dans le cadre du Forum Social Européen de Saint-Denis, en novembre 2003:

● L'impérialisme, le militarisme et la guerre;
● Pouvoirs, contre-pouvoirs, dualité de pouvoir;
● Mouvements sociaux et lutte politique.

Ces tables rondes accorderont une importance particulière aux expériences en cours en Amérique latine.

Il assurera une présence et l'animation de débats dans différentes universités d'été et rencontres organisées pendant l'été 2003.

Il sera présent lors du 4e Forum Social Mondial à Mumbai (Inde) en 2004.

Il tiendra dans le premier semestre 2004 son premier séminaire de travail international sur la question de l'impérialisme et de la guerre, débouchant sur un dossier commun publié dans les différentes langues par les revues associées.

Enfin, il contribuera à la réussite de la tenue, en 2004 également, du 4e Congrès Marx International, organisé à l'initiative de la revue *Actuel Marx*.

Project K will be present at Lausanne in the framework of the meetings of 15 & 16 May against the G8 Summit. It will offer the following three round-tables during the European Social Forum at Saint-Denis in November 2003:

● *Imperialism, militarism and war;*

● *Power, counterpower, and dual power;*

● *Social movements and political struggle.*

These roundtables will pay particular attention to current experiences in Latin America. It will be present, and organise debates, at various summer schools and meetings organised by the European radical left during the summer of 2003.

It will also have a presence at the Fourth World Social Forum in Mumbai (India) in 2004.

In early 2004, it will hold its first international seminar on the question of imperialism and war, which will result in a common dossier that will be published in various languages in the associated journals.

Finally, it will contribute to the successful organisation, also in 2004, of the Fourth International Marx Congress, initiated by the journal Actuel Marx.

Au printemps 2002, les responsables des revues *Viento Sur* (État Espagnol), *Erre* (Italie), *Historical Materialism, International Socialism* (Grande-Bretagne), *Actuel Marx, ContreTemps, Critique Communiste* (France) se sont réunis pour se constituer en réseau européen—dans un premier temps—de publications marxistes critiques.

In the spring of 2002, representatives of the journals Viento Sur *(Spain),* Erre *(Italy),* Historical Materialism, International Socialism *(UK),* Actuel Marx, ContreTemps, *and* Critique Communiste *(France) met in order to constitute a European network—as a first step—of critical Marxist publications.*

Baptisé **Projet K** (comme *Klasse, Kapital, Kampf, Kommunismus*, ou Kafka!), ce projet entend contribuer à internationaliser le renouveau du marxisme critique, en faisant circuler les documents, recherches, et controverses marquantes. Il entend brosser l'air du temps et les modes idéologiques à rebrousse-poil. Enraciné dans les résistances à la mondialisation capitaliste et au nouveau militarisme impérial, il s'efforcera penser l'incertitude du présent dans la tension entre un héritage problématique et un avenir à construire.

Called **Project K** *(as in* Klasse, Kapital, Kampf, Kommunismus, *or* Kafka!), *this project intends to contribute to an internationalisation of the* *renewal of critical Marxism, by circulating texts, research papers and salient controversies. It hopes to brush the spirit of the age and the dominant ideologies against the grain. Rooted in the forms of resistance to capitalist globalisation and to the new imperial militarism, it will try to address the uncertainty of the present through the creative tension between a problematic legacy and future that is yet to be constructed.*

Aussi éloigné de l'illusion de la table rase et de la nouveauté absolue, que des routines dogmatiques, le réseau revendique sa fidélité envers une tradition nourrie des expériences désastreuses du siècle passé, en même temps qu'il affirme son ouverture aux grandes interrogations de l'heure. Il vise ainsi à proposer un lieu de rencontre et de dialogue entre des cultures et des trajectoires différentes, à jeter un point entre engagements militants et recherches universitaires, à créer un lien entre des générations dont l'expérience constitutive diffère, à faire circuler la réflexion entre des espaces de débat trop souvent prisonniers des cloisonnements nationaux ou des rigidités disciplinaires.

Rejecting equally both the illusion of a blank slate or the notion of absolute novelty, and dogmatic routinism, the network affirms its fidelity to a tradition that has been enriched by the experiences of the past century, while simultaneously affirming its openness to the major questions of the current conjuncture. Its aim is to offer a space of encounter and dialogue between different cultures and trajectories, to bridge between activist commitments and academic research, to create a link between generations whose constitutive experiences differ greatly, to help the circulation of ideas between arenas of debate that are too often imprisoned by national provincialism or disciplinary rigidities.

À l'heure où le monde connaît des bouleversements majeurs, où la crise sociale et écologique démontre que le règne du capital se survit au prix d'une irrationalité et d'une violence croissante, où le monde s'installe dans l'état d'exception et de guerre permanente, l'effort pour comprendre ce présent incertain est plus que jamais nécessaire pour passer de la résistance à l'alternative.

In an age when the world is undergoing major transformations, when the social and ecological crisis demonstrates that the reign of capital survives only at the cost of growing irrationality and violence, when the planet is increasingly subjected to a state of exception and permanent warfare, the effort to understand this uncertain present is more than ever necessary in order to pass from resistance to an alternative.

Nous nous sommes fixés un premier programme de travail partant des questions nécessaires à la refondation d'une gauche radicale à la hauteur de défis sociaux, écologiques, culturels, de cette époque. Nous aborderons les chantiers de nouvelles sociologies et des luttes sociales, de l'impérialisme et des souverainetés, des guerres et du militarisme, du marché et des formes de propriété, des totalitarismes et des traditions libertaires, de la fracture écologique ou de la médiatisation du monde, de l'égalité et de l'universalité.

We have set ourselves an initial programme of work by taking as our point of departure those questions that must be addressed if a radical Left is to be refounded that is equal to the social, ecological and cultural challenges of this epoch. We will address issues such as the new sociologies and modes of struggle, imperialism and sovereignties, wars and militarism, the market and property forms, totalitarianisms and libertarian traditions, the ecological divide, the media's penetration of the world, equality and universality.

projetk2002@hotmail.com

Actuel Marx (F)
ActuelMarx@u-paris10.fr
www.penelope.u-paris10.fr/ActuelMarx/

ContreTemps (F)
editionstextuel@wanadoo.fr

Critique Communiste (F)
criticom@lcr-rouge.org
www.lcr-rouge.org

Erre (I)
redazione@erre.info
www.erre.info

Historical Materialism (UK)
hm@lse.ac.uk
www.brill.nl

International Socialism (UK)
isj@swp.org.uk
www.swp.org.uk/isj/isj.htm

Viento Sur (E)
vientosur@nodo50.org
www.vientosur.info

Crying out for revolution

A review of John Holloway, **Change the World Without Taking Power:**
The Meaning of Revolution Today *(Pluto, 2002), £15.99*

MIKE GONZALEZ

For the anti-capitalist movement across the world, the Zapatista rising in Mexico in January 1994 was a kind of symbolic awakening. Although the movement would really reach a point of generalisation with the Seattle demonstrations against the WTO five years later, it looked back into a prehistory that seemed to begin with that indigenous rising in Chiapas. Its scream of defiance—*Ya Basta!*—became a watchword picked up and relayed by a new generation of rebels and resisters.

In some senses, the Zapatistas' symbolic capital arose from the apparent simplicity of their act of resistance. Their wooden rifles and simple dress became iconic—representative of a kind of innocence, a purity of motive that appealed to a generation that wore Che Guevara T-shirts and found its heroes among the uncorrupted voices of the oppressed like Malcolm X and Che. There was a strong moral impulse at the heart of this new kind of politics. And that was, without question, a reaction against a history of Stalinism which had brought Marxism into deep disrepute and through which the revolutionary ideal had been tainted with the recent memory of the Ceausescus and the Brezhnevs and the Hoxhas. They had each employed a grotesque parody of socialist ideas to legitimate their tyrannies.

Yet this new anti-capitalist movement seemed proud to describe itself as revolutionary, as an enemy of a global capitalist system of exploitation and oppression. Today, that movement has swollen and deepened, and added to its vocabulary of denunciation a concept of imperialism it has rediscovered for itself in the developing resistance to the military assault on Iraq.

The scream, to use John Holloway's term, has become deafening.

As it has grown louder, the debate within the movement has begun to move from denunciation and critique to questions of revolution and the construction of a different society. What kind of world is this 'better place', this 'possible place' announced at successive world and European forums? And what are the obstacles that stand in the way of its creation? In the course of that discussion across the global movement, a number of distinct positions are beginning to emerge.[1]

We have dealt extensively in previous editions of this journal and other publications with the view that the existing nation-state can come to reflect and defend the demands for reform. In Europe, this hope is expressed in the campaigns around the Tobin tax—a limited redistributive measure through which some of global capitalism's excesses might be attenuated by a small reduction of corporate profits. In recent months, this aspiration to reform and renegotiate the relative rules of participation in the world system found new reason for optimism with the emergence of what Hugo Chávez, the Venezuelan president, wittily described as 'the axis of good'. The combination of his own regime with the new Brazilian government of Lula and the recently elected Ecuadorean president Lucio Gutiérrez was seen by some commentators as representing a new space for democracy and reform, strong enough to challenge the prevailing norms in international trade. A very few months after Lula's accession to power, however, he is confronting both the left within his own party and large sections of his working class base as he seeks to justify new conditions of austerity imposed by the international financial system.[2]

Large sections of the anti-capitalist movement are rightly sceptical of such views, of course. It does not take much searching through the annals of history to find examples of promises of renovation and reform that have been turned on their head in hours or days. In Britain, France and Spain, for example, social democratic parties promising profound transformations have built alliances with sections of the bourgeoisie against the working class and have enthusiastically assumed the priorities of global capital. The capitalist state is fast proving to a new generation its role in organising and maintaining capitalism itself.

For those without illusions in the capacity of the nation-state to reform itself, who are often among the most resolute fighters against it, a different body of ideas has been offered as a practice and a solution. The hugely successful (and often impenetrable) *Empire*, by Toni Negri and Michael Hardt, has found a keen audience among them. August Nimtz has offered a thorough (and in my view devastating) critique of their views in a recent edition of this journal.[3] But it is interesting to note

Holloway's own critique of Hardt and Negri, and in particular of their central concept of the 'unrooted and amorphous "multitude" that has replaced the industrial proletariat' (as Nimtz puts it).[4] Holloway appears in many ways to agree, in his critique:

> *Worst of all, perhaps, is the total eclipsing of the centrality of doing in the development of the concept of 'multitude'. The concept of 'working class', for all its problems, for all its fetishised deformations, has at least the great merit of taking us to the centrality of human purposive activity, social doing. In the concept of multitude, this is lost completely. If doing is not at the centre of our thought, all that is left is opposition, not hope.*[5]

In his rejection of Hardt and Negri, however, Holloway exposes some of the contradictions in his own thinking as well as setting out the problems of language that sometimes serve to obscure them.

Holloway employs a characteristic and highly idiosyncratic language to express his ideas. A couple of examples:

> *The crystallisation of that-which-has-been-done into a 'thing' shatters the flow of doing into a million fragments. Thing-ness denies the primacy of doing (and hence of humanity).*[6]

or:

> *Identity makes life bearable. Identity kills pain. Identity dulls feeling...identity, that fragmentation that enables us to erect private morality into a wall to keep out the pain of the world. The scream is the recognition and confrontation of social pain.*[7]

There is kind of democratic impulse behind this language—and a poetry that clearly borrows from the lyrical and intensely metaphorical writings of Subcomandante Marcos, the leader of the Zapatistas.[8] But it also bears an embedded critique of the language of scientific interpretation, and a concentration on the subjective as the terrain of revolution.

'It is from rage that thought is born, not from the pose of reason...'[9] That rage becomes 'the scream', which he defines as the negation, an opposition born from instinct or from a sense of other possibilities within us. 'It is not only groups of people that are oppressed', he says, 'but particular aspects of our personality'. The scream comes from those suppressed areas of the self, and is evidence of what other potentialities lie within us all. And the imagined life in which those other parts may find expression is defined by (a term he borrows from Marcos) 'dignity'—the rediscovery of our full humanity.

Where Negri and Hardt suggest that that can be done by an act of physical and social withdrawal from the social relations of production, the creation of other 'free' spaces, Holloway remains too rooted in a Marxist understanding of capitalist production to buy the idea.

Indeed, the new language actually conceals understandings which may be found, often in equally poetic language, in the works of Marx himself. Commodity fetishism, on which Holloway rests so much of his case, was a concept which allowed Marx to address the way in which the world of objects, produced by human labour, then presents itself as a world of things *outside*, and indeed *alien* to the producer. 'Identity', in Holloway's usage of the term, thus becomes a way of describing our equally fixed positions in relation to that world of things—our 'power-to', as he puts it, is subordinated to the 'power-over'. 'Criticism', then, 'is an assault on identity'.[10]

What follows is a kind of caricature of Marx and Marxism on which Holloway's critique largely rests. He describes that relationship with a world of things as a kind of imprisonment from which only a self appointed elite may exclude themselves. That cartoon version of dialectical thought leads then to the critique of the revolutionary party as the substitute for the class. We may all be able to lay hold of examples of such distortions of the revolutionary tradition—the history of Stalinism and at times of Trotskyism offers a plethora of them. But all were predicated on the marginalisation of the working class from the revolutionary process. Yet in the tradition in which we stand, revolution is the *self emancipation of the working class*.

In among Holloway's often imprecise and muddy metaphors it is easy to become confused as to why this is not his purpose too, especially since he frequently makes reference to the centrality of that idea. Yet at the same time he departs from it with an argument at once sophisticated and demobilising. Class, he argues, is the product of capitalist relations of production; we are working class because our labour is alienated. Clearly, the proletariat as a class will disappear, and become the universal class, when alienated production is obliterated. It is not John Holloway who invented the image of human beings overcoming alienation.

But the 'negation' of that alienated self is neither an act of will nor an act of consciousness alone, but a conscious transformation of the material conditions of production. What is lacking in Holloway is the sense of the dialectic, the way in which we are locked into production in conditions which lead to an inescapable contradiction. We are addressed as individuals, yet we are inescapably social; we are shapers of the world who are constantly told that the world is shaped by other forces; we are equals in our common alienation or our shared labour who are relentlessly persuaded of our difference. Far from dissolving the social relations of production into mere economic categories, Marx and

Marxism affirm the opposite—that 'economic categories are only the abstractions of the social relations of production'.[11]

In his difficult discussion of 'identity' Holloway argues that the concept of working class (which as we saw earlier he finds meaningful when contrasted with Hardt and Negri's 'multitude') is fetishised. That class identity encloses us and locks us into a kind of dependency on capitalism—the very capitalism we reject—because we cannot see ourselves as other than workers. Again the problem is a wilful refusal to recognise the decades of Marxist debate in which the working class is the subject of revolution as well as its object.

This leads Holloway into a trap whereby negation becomes an act of will, of psychological redefinition rather than material transformation. We can only engage *socially* in that 'purposive doing' whose highest expression is revolution. A world without private ownership of the means of production is the vision of a propertyless class. Its achievement, however, is not merely an act of affirmation but the culmination of class struggle. How is freedom to be achieved, other than by wresting power from those who impose unfreedom, who have 'power-over'?

Holloway is scathing in his critique of *Empire* of the notion that alternative spaces can be created—be they nations or communities. Yet his alternative to 'power-over', his unfetishised space, is a metaphorical space. This place of 'constant becoming', located somewhere outside history, is designed, I imagine, to avoid the difficult question of what to do about the capitalist class and its machinery of domination and control. Fetishism, he says, is 'in antagonism to the opposing movement of anti-fetishisation, the struggle to reunite subject and object, to recompose doing and done'.[12]

Yet the struggle for that freedom is in the first instance a material battle to wrest control of the means of production from the controlling class. It is true that labour is alienated under conditions of capitalist production; but it is also true that that powerlessness is also a power. Without labour there can be no production. That is the contradiction from which the development of class consciousness emerges and on which the power of workers rests.

Hal Draper contrasts two visions of freedom. The first (the anarchist) depends on the 'total impermissibility of any imposition of any authority upon the unconditional autonomy of the sovereign Ego'. The second, Marx's view, 'depends upon the relation of the individual to his (or her) membership in the human species which is historically organised in a society... It is a shorthand term for democratic freedom in society'.[13]

I began this review with a mention of the Zapatistas. In some senses, the material reality of their situation is the living expression of the limitations of the autonomist position that Holloway argues. The symbolic authority of Chiapas is boundless, the internal life of the communities driven by the highest and most noble ideals of authentic co-operation and community, the language of political life grounded in multiplicity and the popular imagination. Yet consider their conditions of life—besieged by a ruthless global capital, the very stuff of life (water, electricity, medicines) repeatedly taken from them, the state machine squeezing them in a menacing vice. Beyond the steel cordon lie their allies and supporters, reproducing the power of capital. The Zapatistas gave the anti-capitalist movement a dream of freedom and a language of liberation; yet the power to realise the project, to seize the state and make the revolution, still lies elsewhere.

Notes

1 See A Callinicos, 'State of Discontent', in *Socialist Review*, March 2003, pp11-13.
2 See M Gonzalez, 'Brazil in the Eye of the Storm', in *International Socialism* 98 (Spring 2003), pp57-76.
3 A Nimtz, 'Class struggle Under "Empire": In Defence of Marx and Engels', in *International Socialism* 96 (Autumn 2002), pp47-70.
4 Ibid, p49.
5 J Holloway, 'Time to Revolt: Reflections on Empire', October 2002, published on The Commoner website at www.commoner.org.uk
6 J Holloway, *Change the World Without Taking Power* (London, 2002), p33.
7 Ibid, p103.
8 See J Holloway and E Peláez (eds), *Zapatista!* (London, 1998), and in particular the editors' introduction, 'Reinventing Revolution'.
9 J Holloway, *Change the World Without Taking Power*, op cit, p1.
10 Ibid, p106.
11 A Callinicos, *The Revolutionary Ideas of Karl Marx* (London, 1987), p75.
12 J Holloway, *Change the World Without Taking Power*, op cit, p89.
13 H Draper, *Karl Marx's Theory of Revolution*, vol 4 (New York, 1990), pp174-175.

Philosophy and the masses

*A review of Stathis Kouvelakis, **Philosophy and Revolution: From Kant to Marx** (Verso, 2003), £17*

MARK THOMAS

Is Marxism simply an insightful way of looking at capitalism, or does it possess a plausible strategy for transforming society?

In the late 1990s there was a certain revived interest in Marx. But this was Marx as the great critic of the anarchy of capitalist production. This was the time of the Asian economic crisis, and even free market apologists were thrown into panic and talked of 'the end of capitalism'. But Marx's communism and advocacy of working class revolution remained derided and dismissed.[1] The argument was that Marx's political project was not to be taken seriously in the wake of the collapse of the regimes in Eastern Europe. Theory and practice were thus kept at arm's length. You can use Marx to analyse capitalism, but don't attempt to change it.

In fact, the claim that Marx had no coherent theory of politics was one of the central themes in the onslaught on Marxism in the late 1970s. The alleged role Marx gives to the economy leaves no space for human intervention in the realm of politics, and Marx's emphasis on society over the individual leads to a rejection of the classical issues concerning liberal political thinkers, namely justice, rights, and so on. The argument runs that this paves the way for totalitarianism, where an all-powerful state annihilates the individual.[2]

Stathis Kouvelakis's *Philosophy and Revolution* has the great merit of taking Marx's political project seriously. It traces the emergence of Marxism through a careful study of the evolution and development of Marx's ideas as a young German radical in the 1840s, when Marx was still in his twenties. Marx was not born a Marxist, but by the mid-1840s the new theory of historical materialism was sketched out in fundamentals at least, and Marx, together with Frederick Engels, had embarked on a lifelong commitment to revolutionary socialism. How did this happen? Why did Marxism emerge in this precise period and manner?

Germany in the 1840s

In Marx's youth Germany was still a patchwork of small states under the hegemony of Prussian absolutism. It was mired in backwardness, yet with a feudalism already breaking down under the impact of new social relationships associated with the rise of a new form of society, capitalism. Caught between the old world and the new, German society was dominated by the question of its relationship to its French neighbour, or more precisely to that country's great revolution. Was the French Revolution of 1789 Germany's future?

Reactionaries were, of course, hostile to everything the French Revolution stood for, and to the whole tradition of the Enlightenment which had preceded it. But the response of the majority of German intellectuals who detested this stultifying old order was not a simple desire to repeat the experience. From Immanuel Kant onwards, they defended the French Revolution against the reactionaries, but they outlined a different path for Germany, a road to modernity that would avoid revolution. Thus they were plagued by a desire to reap the gains of the French Revolution, the abolition of feudalism and so on, but without unleashing the mass upsurge from below that had been at the heart of the French experience. 'Revolution without revolution' was the first hallmark of the 'German road'. How would this be attained? Quite simply, it would be philosophy that would offer the prospect of reaping the fruits of the French Revolution without its traumas and risks. The realm of ideas allied to a reforming state would supplant the role of the masses. Kouvelakis puts it like this:

> The revolution is legitimate, but it is other people's business; the mission of 'spiritualisation' incumbent on Germany will allow it to escape the horrors of the revolutionary hell even as it reaps the benefits of revolutionary gains; thanks to state reform, stimulated by the practical philosophy that has invested the public sphere, it will prove possible to resolve existing contradictions peacefully and productively, and so on.[3]

Nor was this accidental. It reflected the weakness of the German bourgeoisie and the threat from below. Kouvelakis argues that Kant, for example, 'both fears and...deems utopian' any repeat of the revolutionary mass mobilisations of the 1790s.[4] Both fears and deems utopian? At first glance these might appear contradictory responses. After all, to be a danger the revolution must at least be a feasible prospect, and if it is an impossibility then why feel threatened by it?

But from a class perspective it falls into place. The German bourgeoisie is too weak to overthrow Prussian absolutism on the model of its French counterpart. But it is already beginning to fear a working class breathing down its neck which is stronger than that of 1789. In other words, the 'German road', the hope for a 'revolution without revolution', modernisation from above through reforms is rooted in the historical situation the German bourgeoisie found itself in. A victorious German bourgeois revolution is utopian, but any attempt might trigger something altogether more radical from below. In 1848 this is of course what happens, when the bourgeoisie takes fright and turns back to the arms of reaction.

Central to this attempt to construct a 'German road' avoiding revolution is that intellectuals like Kant abstain from engaging in agitation for radical change among the masses. Self censorship will maintain the divide between intellectuals and the mass of the population—to the point even of cultivating a deliberately obscure style. Philosophy will address only the king and an 'educated' property-owing public. This carefully limited public arena is to serve as a *substitute* for revolution in the hope that it will foster a reforming, rational spirit in the state.[5] In return Kant asks that the state tolerate this circumscribed debate, and hopes that it will take the advice of the philosophers and begin a process of reform from above. This gap between philosophy (intellectuals) and the masses, between theory and practice, is the second hallmark of the majority of German radicals from Kant through to Marx's contemporaries (and Marx himself, initially).

Kant's quandary is that he recognises that this strategy may well fail. What if Prussian absolutism remains immune to the call of the philosophers, and revolution erupts instead? It is precisely this fear that turns into a reality in the 1840s. In 1840 a new Prussian king, Friedrich Wilhelm IV, meant new hopes for progress. These were rapidly dashed. Press freedom was quashed, and the followers of a radical interpretation of Hegel (the 'young Hegelians') were pushed out of the universities. By 1842-1843 the democratic movement in Germany was sharply confronted with a crisis, as the new monarchy turned to repression. Any hope of reform was put paid to:

> *By unambiguously dashing hopes that he would liberalise the Prussian regime, Friedrich Wilhelm IV succeeded in rapidly deepening the crisis, in a double sense: eliminating any possibility that the regime might reform itself,*

he made it inevitable that its contradictions would burst into the open; but, by the same token, he destabilised an opposition whose entire strategy had been predicated, precisely, on the calculation that an out and out conflict could be avoided.[6]

If you look to the state to reform itself to avoid the prospect of social revolution, how do you respond if that same state sets its face against any modernisation, precisely because it fears any reforms will inevitably open the door to revolution? At this point the German democratic movement entered into crisis. From this period on the Young Hegelians are riven by polarisation and fragmentation. Bruno Bauer, once the key figure and Marx's mentor, together with his Berlin coterie, 'the Free' retreat from all political engagement, blaming the masses for not rising in support of the philosophers in the face of this repression. They instead champion an idealist and elitist 'critical criticism' as the only adequate response. Marx savages this in 'The Holy Family', his first collaboration with Frederick Engels in 1844 (although Engels only makes a small contribution to the final text).

'True' socialism

More important than Bauer and 'the Free' is the response of Moses Hess, who turned to a 'philosophical communism' that formed the basis of what Marx and Engels call 'True' socialism in *The Communist Manifesto*. This was probably the dominant current among German radicals on the eve of the 1848 revolutions that swept both Germany and most of Europe. Indeed, Kouvelakis stresses that these ideas held a strong sway inside the workers' movement of the 1840s, not least among the German emigre workers in Paris who formed the League of the Just. It took a protracted struggle for Marx and Engels to win the battle against the ideas of Hess and 'True' socialism. *The Communist Manifesto* comments that 'True' socialism 'spread like an epidemic' in the 1840s.[7]

The 'True' socialists looked for a new principle to act as a substitute for revolution in Germany. Hess wished to 'appropriate the results of the French Revolution peacefully'.[8] This principle or concept is that of the 'social' or 'social-ism', which is to play the role of an alternative to both liberal individualism and revolution.[9] Following the pioneer utopian socialist, Saint Simon, society for Hess was possessed of an underlying, intrinsic harmony. This had been temporarily obscured by the competitive laws of the market which fostered a war of all against all. The task was to rectify this situation and reveal the inner truth of this innate human bond, that is to say 'True' socialism. Hess converts Saint Simon into the language of German philosophy.

In *The European Triarchy*, written in 1841 in the flush of optimism about prospects for change in Germany, Hess clearly identified the Prussian state as the vehicle for introducing this programme of what Kouvelakis aptly describes as 'top-down reform'.[10] Indeed, Hess contrasts the state's 'supreme power...to regulate the spiritual, the physical, and the ethical in society' with an elitist disdain for the masses, 'The multitude has always been uncultivated'. This fear of the masses who are seen as always open to manipulation by reaction 'haunted the pages of *The European Triarchy*, as it did almost all of the Young Hegelians'.[11]

But in response to the crisis in the democratic movement, and the closing of the road of reform, Hess, like Bruno Bauer, engaged in what Kouvelakis calls 'retreat disguised as philosophical offensive'. Hess now declared that the form of government is irrelevant and therefore there is no need to confront the state. Instead he puts forward an increasingly anti-political concept of the 'social'. Simultaneously, socialism and communism are purged of any association with the proletariat.[12] This is the outlook of a socialist humanism aiming at class reconciliation, not revolution. For Hess, communism is the expression of a principle, not of a class interest.

How will this principle triumph? Through education and gradual change. This will allow the triumph of the true essence of humanity, namely love. This transcends class boundaries, overcoming the alienation of capitalists as much as proletarians from a world of money, competition and exploitation. Kouvelakis summarises the political stakes at issue between the 'True' socialists and those like Marx who turned towards revolution: 'The main bone of contention was the question of humanism: class struggle or the dialectic of the human essence; revolution or ethical sermonizing and peaceful propaganda'.[13]

What kind of revolution?

By contrast with Moses Hess, Kouvelakis explores the work of the German poet Heinrich Heine.[14] For Kouvelakis he forms a crucial link between the generation of Hegel and the young radicals of the generation of the 1840s, and he sees in Heine a vital precursor to Marx.

Heine set himself against those who wished the French Revolution to be over, done and dusted, and safely relegated to the past. Heine shunned any craving for harmony, social peace and political moderation.[15]

The central question here was the relationship any new revolution would have to 1789. For Heine it was not simply a question of repeating 1789 but looking to a new revolutionary wave even more radical than its forerunner. For Kouvelakis, Heine is the true initiator of the Young Hegelians and the interpretation of Hegel's thought as revolutionary. He imbues classical idealism with the French spirit—the heritage, in other words, of the French Revolution. Thus he looked to a Franco-German alliance as the key to the future revolution, one that would combine German philosophy and the French revolutionary experience. Theory and practice would at last be united.

The relationship between the past and present also preoccupies Heine's work. He challenges the amnesia of bourgeois society, which sought to deny its birth on the barricades and lived only in a present without any reference to history. Heine saw conflict brewing beneath the surface of the Orleanist regime which had confiscated the French Revolution of 1830.[16] He counterposed antagonism to harmony. But he also challenged traditional republicans who simply repeated the slogans of the past and focused solely on the nature of the political regime— monarchy or republic. However, Heine did not draw from this conclusion an approach that dismissed all political questions in favour of a purely social transformation:

> The bourgeoisie will before all things have order and protection of the laws of property—needs which a republic can satisfy as well as a kingdom. But these shopkeepers know...by instinct that a republic today would not represent the principles of 1789, but only the form under which a new and unheard-of reign of proletarians would realise all the dogmas of the community of property.[17]

Heine's goal was to preserve the 'spirit' rather than just the letter of the French Revolution. Heine was attentive to the altered context of France and Germany in the 1840s—above all the rise of a new force, the proletariat, and the increasingly explosive contradictions of bourgeois society that the French Revolution had left unresolved. It was not enough to simply repeat the old republican formulas—to do so now carried the danger of aiding reaction by not addressing questions of property and equality. So, neither a denial of the past nor its simple repetition rose to the needs of a new historical period.

These, then, are the themes thrown up by Heine's reflections on the nature of the forthcoming revolution—antagonism over reconciliation, the need for any new revolution to go beyond the limits of 1789 and address the 'social' question, but without falling into an apolitical retreat from confronting the state. The idea that the new revolution must be both a political act and a social transformation was at the centre of Marx's inheritance from Heine. The 'revolution is one and indivisible', as Heine put it.

Marx and a new conception of politics

Lenin famously described Marxism as the outcome of a synthesis between German philosophy, French politics and English political economy.[18] Central to Kouvelakis's approach is the claim that this insight only takes us so far. As he successfully shows in his 'group portrait' of German radicals of the 1830s and 1840s, some attempt to combine these elements was almost a common sense in this milieu.[19] Yet those who were to evolve into revolutionaries were a distinct minority.

Kouvelakis structures his book around a contrast between Heinrich Heine and Karl Marx on the one hand, and Moses Hess and the young Frederick Engels on the other.[20] The latter are presented as representatives of 'True' socialism, while Heine and Marx are by contrast the minority current which lays the basis for the theory of a new revolution which preserves the 'spirit' of the French Revolution while going beyond it—a proletarian revolution.

The upshot of this is to demonstrate that Marx's specific way of combining these elements is unique, and represents as much a radical break from all three traditions as any simple synthesis. That this was the case is amply shown by Marx's subsequent polemics with those who hadn't made the break from these traditions, for example Proudhon and French socialism or the various 'Young Hegelians', in *The German Ideology*. Behind this lies the gulf separating Marxism from all forms of liberalism. This, then, is a claim for the novelty of Marx's conception of communism—it is not just a question of taking over pre-existing traditions and combining them, but of a sharp break.

Kouvelakis charts Marx's development from a reformist outlook that assigned a pivotal role to a free press (Marx was editor of a radical bourgeois newspaper in this period, the *Neue Rheinische Zeitung*) to a revolutionary perspective and the birth of a new worldview. In particular Kouvelakis emphasises that this process is a politically driven one for the young Marx, and at the same time involves the emergence of a radically new conception of politics itself.

To begin with Marx, like all the other Young Hegelians, operates within the framework of the 'German road' of reform not revolution. Yet from the outset Marx saw a much more active and engaged role for philosophy. Like Kant, he demanded a public sphere outside the control of absolutism that could conduct a campaign for democratic reform. But Marx aims for a situation in which 'philosophy becomes worldly and the world became philosophical'. [21]

He even calls on philosophy to 'become a newspaper correspondent'! Here is an aspiration for philosophy to overcome its separation from the world of practice. It also breaches the self censorship advocated by Kant. By its nature a newspaper has a greater audience than a philosophical tract. Of course, the very real censorship of the Prussian state still had to be negotiated.

Marx also takes a far more critical approach to Hegel's view of the state. Initially he still accepted the premise that the state's role is to reconcile the conflicts which threaten to tear civil society—the world of the market, private property, competition, and so on—apart. Marx, however, is highly sceptical of Hegel's account of the mechanisms and institutions that will perform the role of overcoming these conflicts. For example, Hegel rejects the argument for representative democracy, and instead talks of 'corporations' which organise the various classes or 'estates' in society. It is these corporations that are to be represented in the state rather than individuals directly. In other words, he gives an inbuilt advantage to the landowning aristocracy, who as an 'estate' are guaranteed a political weight way beyond their actual numbers. Hegel also saw the state civil service as an embodiment of the 'universal'—in other words, the public interest. For Marx these are false solutions—they are 'sham meditations'. From the outset Marx looks to a democratisation of the state, but of the existing state at this point.

But the crisis beginning in 1842-1843 as the Prussian state turned to repression closed off this option. Marx now looked again at the relationship between civil society and the state. What is at stake is nothing less than the question of revolution. Kouvelakis insists that behind this theoretical shift is a political radicalisation. It is not a question of purely abstract intellectual enquiry, but a product of the double crisis of absolutism and reformism in Germany in 1842-1843. But neither can it be seen simply as a reflection of these new circumstances, because only a minority of existing radicals go over to the side of revolution. Thus Kouvelakis sees Marx's shift as a *political act* in the 'heat of battle': 'Before discovering the proletariat, before forging the concept of his theory of history, Marx makes the leap; he is virtually the only one in the democratic German opposition to do so, with the exception...of Heine'.[22]

So Marx becomes a revolutionary before he becomes a Marxist. He now calls for the battle for democracy in Germany to be openly joined. He rejects any attempt to solve the crisis that evades this question, as the 'True' socialists argue.[23]

Marx now moves to settle accounts with both Hegel and the French Revolution. Marx engages in what Kouvelakis describes as a Hegelian critique of Hegel. Marx sees Hegel as failing to deliver on the promise of his own dialectic. Instead of uncovering the real and ceaseless movement of history, it ends up accommodating to empirical reality—the actually existing Prussian state. So, what comes to pass in history turns out simply to be what already exists. The revolutionary promise of Hegel's idealist dialectic turns out to be a conservative justification of the status quo.[24]

Marx then proceeds to launch a critique of the notion of representative government itself. Crucially, this centres on the fact that even this—the maximum possible democracy under capitalism—fails to overcome the division between civil society and the state. The state under representative democracy claims to treat everybody as an equal citizen, yet in the realm of private property the division between the propertied and propertyless remain. Indeed, the state itself is a product of those divisions. Without a state, this polarisation of wealth threatens to explode. The state doesn't 'reconcile' these divisions, it entrenches them:

> *The state is incapable of substantially affecting the contents of civil society, for it is, precisely, a product of civil society's abstraction from itself. Hence the state can overcome social differences only in imaginary ways, in the heaven of the equality that prevails between the subjects of the law.* [25]

So any revolution that fails to eradicate the cleavage between civil society and the state must fall short of real human emancipation, however much it might succeed in democratising the existing state:

> *A revolution is not radical unless it puts an end to the separation between civil society and the state—that is to say, unless it simultaneously overcomes the internal division of civil society and imaginary transcendence of that division, namely the abstraction of the merely political state.* [26]

Bourgeois property and the modern state are two sides of the same coin. They are mutually interdependent. So you cannot, as the 'True' socialists argued, transform bourgeois society without addressing the question of the state. But nor will a purely 'political' revolution suffice. You cannot, says Marx, 'leave the pillars of the house standing'. The revolution must be simultaneously political and social.

So, politics is central to Marx's thought. His ideas are formed in a fight against the apolitical notions of the 'True' socialists, but it is a new way of thinking about politics that cannot be separated from the 'social'. Kouvelakis, somewhat abstractly, calls this a 'transformation of the political that amounts to posing it as a power of transformation'. [27]

There are two related points here. First, Marx is seeking to abolish a view of politics as a separate autonomous sphere. Politics cannot be viewed as a distinct entity from economics or the 'social'. Such a view is a central feature of liberalism. Second, for Marx, overcoming the division of politics and economics is part of the process of establishing truly democratic control from below over the organisation of society. Abolishing politics as a separate sphere is to subject it to conscious human control. Politics will no longer be an alienated realm offering only a fictitious equality and democracy even under representative democracy, but 'truly democratic'.

Kouvelakis's book, while very rich and suggestive, is also demanding and at points slightly ambiguous. It is not always clear whether he believes the state will continue to exist under communism. So he says on the one hand, that the 'state "disappears"—but only as a separate entity, a fixed, immutable given—in order to dissolve into the network of mediations that constitute concrete universality'. But he then insists, 'The "disappearance" of the political state does not in any way signify the pure and simple absence of law, a constitution, or even state institutions. Marx is resistant to "anarchist temptations".'[28]

Perhaps the tightly focused nature of Kouvelakis's book is a hindrance. He only takes the story of Marx's development up to 1844. It might be argued that Marx himself is still ambiguous in what he is saying at this point. Either way, a discussion of Marx's response to the Paris Commune (mentioned in passing) or to the rich tradition of soviets or workers' councils thrown up repeatedly in revolutionary situations in the 20th century would perhaps serve to clarify the issues at stake here. Kouvelakis's argument about Marx's turn to revolution as a political act also provokes some questions. If he is saying that it must be seen as the product of Marx's engagement in the struggle, and not simply as an abstract theoretical development, that seems clear and right. But when he also insists it cannot be interpreted in 'sociological' terms and that Marx's breakthrough to the new perspective 'surges up out of the contradiction', then is there not a danger of saying that it has no relationship to real struggles, to the objective world?

This aside, *Philosophy and Revolution* is a welcome return to the question of Marx's political project. It is a robust defence of Marx's profound concern with the issue of democracy. Given the renewal of the movement against capitalism, this is certainly timely. In particular, Marx's attention to the limits of even representative democracy (remarkably, one written in the 1840s when genuine parliamentary democracy was still only an aspiration) has a real force at a time when the hollow nature of parliamentary democracy has rarely been more apparent.

Marxism was formed at a time of crisis, and the resulting radicalisation of a wing of a movement that had initially sought reform, not revolution. Kouvelakis's insistence that a central part of this process was a confrontation with 'True' socialists who were indifferent to questions of the state and politics has something real and urgent to say to those today seeking a way to successfully challenge capitalism.

Notes

1   J Rees,'The Return of Marx', *International Socialism* 79 (Summer 1998).
2   Gareth Stedman Jones's introduction to the new Penguin edition of the *The Communist Manifesto* (London, 2002) reiterates this liberal critique of Marx (p179). Indeed, Stedman Jones only reserves any praise for Marx's famous celebration of the revolutionary dynamism of the capitalist system (p5).
3   S Kouvelakis, *Philosophy and Revolution,* (London, 2003), p274.
4   Ibid, p14.
5   Ibid, p19.
6   Ibid, p145.
7   K Marx and F Engels, *The Communist Manifesto*, op cit, p251.
8   S Kouvelakis, op cit, p141.
9   Ibid, p131.
10   Ibid, p143.
11   Ibid, see pp141-144.
12   Ibid, p153.
13   Ibid, p165.
14   Heinrich Heine (1797-1856) is perhaps best known among socialists for the poem 'The Silesian Weavers', written after the 1844 uprising of the weavers. The poem can be found in *Heinrich Heine* (London, 1997). Testimony to his radicalism is the fact that Hitler, after occupying Paris, ordered the poet's grave at Montmartre to be destroyed.
15   Ibid, p45.
16   In July 1830 revolution broke out in France after the last Bourbon king, Charles X, had attempted to suppress the liberal press. It ended in the establishment of the 'bourgeois monarchy' under Louis-Philippe, from the rival Orleanist dynastic house contending for the French crown.
17   Heinrich Heine, quoted in S Kouvelakis, op cit, p60.
18   See V I Lenin, 'The Three Sources and Three Component Parts of Marxism', in V I Lenin, *Marx, Engels, Marxism* (Beijing, 1978).
19   For example, the very title of Moses Hess's *The European Triarchy* reflects his attempt to distil a synthesis of English, French and German experiences, in this case to find a path for evading revolution.
20   Kouvelakis argues that the young Frederick Engels was highly influenced by Moses Hess, and was a 'True' socialist prior to his 'real encounter' with Karl Marx. Kouvelakis interprets Engels' *The Condition of the Working Class in England* as a 'True' socialist text. This seems to me to 'bend the stick' far too hard, to say the least. Too many hostages are being offered to the argument that counterposes Engels to Marx, and sees in the former the source of the mechanical Marxism prevalent in the Second International. An account of how Engels—and not just Marx, who after all was also strongly influenced by Hess for a time—makes the transition to a consistent revolutionary outlook might reveal a more rounded perspective on the young Engels' break from 'True' socialism. For a different perspective, see 'The Revolutionary Ideas of Frederick Engels', *International Socialism* 65 (Winter 1994).
21   Ibid, p259.

22   Ibid, p278.

23   Stedman Jones describes the section in *The Communist Manifesto* on 'True' socialism as 'sectarian'. Yet surely it was the tendency of some 'True' socialists to turn their fire on those fighting for democracy on the eve on the 1848 revolutions that was both sectarian and reactionary, however radical the rhetoric was that cloaked it. Marx and Engels' polemic insisted that socialists took part in the fight for democracy even while they sought to extend into a struggle for socialism. This is one of their most important contributions to the revolutionary tradition. See, for example, August Nimtz's excellent treatment of this question in A Nimtz, *Marx and Engels: Their Contribution to the Democratic Breakthrough* (Albany, 2000).

24   S Kouvelakis, op cit, pp288-292. See also J Rees, *The Algebra of Revolution* (New Jersey, 1998), for one of the clearest approaches to Marx's relationship to Hegel.

25   S Kouvelakis, op cit, p300.

26   Ibid, p326.

27   Ibid, p310.

28   Ibid, pp309-310.

The Socialist Workers Party is one of an international grouping of socialist organisations:

AUSTRALIA	International Socialist Organisation, PO Box A338, Sydney South. *iso@iso.org.au*
AUSTRIA	Linkswende, Postfach 87, 1108 Wien. *linkswende@yahoo.com*
BRITAIN	Socialist Workers Party, PO Box 82, London E3 3LH. *enquiries@swp.org.uk*
CANADA	International Socialists, PO Box 339, Station E, Toronto, Ontario M6H 4E3. *iscanada@on.aibn.com*
CYPRUS	Ergatiki Demokratia, PO Box 27280, Nicosia. *wd@workersdemocracy.net*
CZECH REPUBLIC	Socialisticka Solidarita, PO Box 1002, 11121 Praha 1. *socsol@email.cz*
DENMARK	Internationale Socialister, PO Box 5113, 8100 Aarhus C. *intsoc@socialister.dk*
FINLAND	Sosialistiliitto, PL 288, 00171 Helsinki. *info@sosialistiliitto.org*
FRANCE	Socialisme par en bas, BP 15-94111, Arcueil Cedex. *contact@socialismeparenbas.org*
GERMANY	Linksruck, Postfach 44 0346, 12003 Berlin. *info@linksruck.de*
GHANA	International Socialist Organisation, PO Box TF202, Trade Fair, Labadi, Accra. *isogh@hotmail.com*
GREECE	Sosialistiko Ergatiko Komma, c/o Workers Solidarity, PO Box 8161, Athens 100 10. *sek@otenet.gr*
HOLLAND	Internationale Socialisten, PO Box 92025, 1090AA Amsterdam. *info@internationalesocialisten.org*
IRELAND	Socialist Workers Party, PO Box 1648, Dublin 8. *swp@clubi.ie*
ITALY	Comunismo dal Basso, Leeder, CP Bologna, Succ 5. *dalbasso@hotmail.com*
NEW ZEALAND	Socialist Workers Organisation, PO Box 13-685, Auckland. *socialist-worker@pl.net*
NORWAY	Internasjonale Socialisterr, Postboks 9226, Grønland, 0134 Oslo. *intsos@intsos.no*
POLAND	Pracownicza Demokracja, PO Box 12, 01-900 Warszawa 118. *pracdem@go2.pl*
SPAIN	En Lucha, Apartado 563, 08080 Barcelona. *info@enlucha.org*
UNITED STATES	Left Turn, PO Box 445, New York, NY 10159-0445. *leftturn@leftturn.org*
URUGUAY	Izquierda Revolucionaria. *ir@adinet.com.uy*
ZIMBABWE	International Socialist Organisation, PO Box 6758, Harare. *isozim@hotmail.com*

The following issues of *International Socialism* (second series) are available price £3 (including postage) from IS Journal, PO Box 82, London E3 3LH. *International Socialism* 2:58 and 2:65 are available on cassette from the Royal National Institute for the Blind (Peterborough Library Unit). Phone 01733 370 777.

International Socialism 2:98 Spring 2003
Sam Ashman: The anti-capitalist movement and the war ★ John Rees: Cairo calling ★ The Cairo Declaration ★ Colin Sparks: Inside the media ★ Mike Gonzalez: In the eye of the storm ★ Robert Sáenz and Isidoro Cruz Bernal: The driving force behind the 'Argentinazo' ★ Rachel Aldred: Between the no longer and the not yet ★ Dave Renton: When superpowers lose ★ Hassan Mahamdallie: Defying the colour line ★ John Rose: The Jubilee and the Apocalypse ★ Jane Hardy: Toil and trouble: the state of the US economy ★

International Socialism 2:97 Winter 2002
Alex Callinicos: The grand strategy of the American empire ★ Murray Smith: Where is the SWP going? ★ Nick McKerrell: The united front today ★ John Rees: The broad party, the revolutionary party and the united front ★ Gilbert Achcar: Engels: theorist of war, theorist of revolution ★ Dave Crouch: The inevitability of radicalism ★ Sheila McGregor: Neither Washington nor Moscow ★

International Socialism 2:96 Autumn 2002
Chris Harman: The workers of the world ★ August Nimtz: Class struggle under 'Empire': in defence of Marx and Engels ★ John Bellamy Foster: Marx's ecology in historical perspective ★ Mike Kidron: Failing growth and rampant costs: two ghosts in the machine of modern capitalism ★ Ian Birchall: Zola for the 21st century ★ Jim Wolfreys: The disposable heroes of hypocrisy ★

International Socialism 2:95 Summer 2002
Hassan Mahamdallie: Racism: myths and realities ★ Jim Wolfreys: 'The centre cannot hold': fascism, the left and the crisis of French politics ★ Daniel Bensaïd: Leaps! Leaps! Leaps! ★ Slavoj Zizek: A cyberspace Lenin—why not? ★ John Rees: Leninism in the 21st century ★ Anne Alexander: Redrawing the political map ★ Sam Ashman: Islam and imperialism ★ Megan Trudell: From *tangentopoli* to Genoa ★

International Socialism 2:94 Spring 2002
Chris Harman: Argentina: rebellion at the sharp end of the world crisis ★ Martin Smith: The return of the rank and file? ★ Leo Zeilig: Crisis in Zimbabwe ★ Jim Wolfreys: Pierre Bourdieu: voice of resistance ★ Richard Greeman: Memoirs of a revolutionary ★ Dave Crouch: The seeds of national liberation ★

International Socialism 2:93 Special issue
John Rees: Imperialism: globalisation, the state and war ★ Jonathan Neale: The long torment of Afghanistan ★ Anne Alexander: The crisis in the Middle East ★ Mike Gonzalez: The poisoned embrace: Plan Colombia and the expansion of imperial power ★ Chris Harman: The new world recession ★

International Socialism 2:92 Autumn 2001
Tom Behan: 'Nothing can be the same again' ★ Boris Kagarlitsky: The road from Genoa ★ Alex Callinicos: Toni Negri in perspective ★ Jack Fuller: The new workerism: the politics of the Italian autonomists ★ Goretti Horgan: How does globalisation affect women? ★ Rumy Hasan: East Asia since the 1997 crisis ★ Charlie Kimber: Dark heart of imperialism ★ Megan Trudell: The pursuit of 'unbounded freedom' ★

International Socialism 2:91 Summer 2001
Susan George: What now? ★ Walden Bello: The global conjuncture ★ Chris Nineham: An idea whose time has come ★ Mike Marqusee: Labour's long march to the right ★ Mike Davis: Wild streets—*American Graffiti* versus the Cold War ★ Goretti Horgan: Changing women's lives in Ireland ★ John Lister: We will fight them in the hedgerows ★ Mike Gonzalez: The Zapatistas after the Great March—a postscript ★ Dragan Plavsic: Hoist on their own petards ★

International Socialism 2:90 Spring 2001
John Rees: Anti-capitalism, reformism and socialism ★ Chris Harman: Beyond the boom ★ Walden Bello: 2000: the year of global protest ★ Michael Lavalette and others: The woeful record of the House of Blair ★ Brian Manning: History and socialism ★ Peter Morgan: A troublemaker's charter ★

International Socialism 2:89 Winter 2000
Lindsey German: Serbia's spring in October ★ Anne Alexander: Powerless in Gaza: the Palestinian Authority and the myth of the 'peace process' ★ Boris Kagarlitsky: The lessons of Prague ★ Mike Gonzalez: The Zapatistas: the challenges of revolution in a new millennium ★ Stuart Hood: Memoirs of the Italian Resistance ★ Esme Choonara: Threads of resistance ★ Megan Trudell: Setting the record straight ★ Judy Cox: Reasons to be cheerful: theories of anti-capitalism ★ Mark O'Brien: A comment on *Tailism and the Dialectic* ★

International Socialism 2:88 Autumn 2000
Chris Harman: Anti-capitalism: theory and practice ★ Paul McGarr: Why green is red ★ Boris Kagarlitsky: The suicide of *New Left Review* ★ Gilbert Achcar: The 'historical pessimism' of Perry Anderson ★ Dave Renton: Class consciousness and the origins of Labour ★ Keith Flett: Socialists and the origins of Labour: some other perspectives ★ John Newsinger: Fantasy and revolution: an interview with China Miéville ★

International Socialism 2:87 Summer 2000
Lindsey German: How Labour lost its roots ★ Mark O'Brien: Socialists and the origins of Labour ★ Judy Cox: Skinning a live tiger paw by paw ★ Peter Morgan: The morning after the night before... ★ John Newsinger: Plumbing the depths: some recent books on New Labour ★ Abbie Bakan: From Seattle to Washington: the making of a movement ★ Jim Wolfreys: In perspective: Pierre Bourdieu ★ Nick Barrett: Complement to 'Reformism and class polarisation in Europe' ★ Mark Krantz: Humanitarian intentions on the road to hell ★ John Rees: Tony Cliff: theory and practice ★ Ygal Sarneh: A revolutionary life ★ Shaun Doherty: The language of liberation ★

International Socialism 2:86 Spring 2000
John Charlton: Talking Seattle ★ Abbie Bakan: After Seattle: the politics of the World Trade Organisation ★ Mark O'Brien: In perspective: Susan George ★ Rob Ferguson: Chechnya: the empire strikes back ★ Lindsey German: The Balkans' imperial problem ★ Megan Trudell: The Russian civil war: a Marxist analysis ★ Robin Blackburn: Reviewing the millennia ★ Jim Wolfreys: In defence of Marxism ★ Judy Cox: Can capitalism be sustained? ★

International Socialism 2:85 Winter 1999
Alex Callinicos: Reformism and class polarisation in Europe ★ Michael Lavalette and Gerry Mooney: New Labour, new moralism: the welfare politics and ideology of New Labour under Blair ★ Ken Coates: Benign imperialism versus United Nations ★ John Baxter: Is the UN an alternative to 'humanitarian imperialism'? ★ John Rose: Jesus: history's most famous missing person ★ Chris Harman: The 20th century: an age of extremes or an age of possibilities? ★ Mike Gonzalez: Is modernism dead? ★ Peter Morgan: The man behind the mask ★ Anne Alexander: All power to the imagination ★ Anna Chen: George Orwell: a literary Trotskyist? ★ Rob Hoveman: History of theory ★ Chris Harman: Comment on Molyneux on art ★

International Socialism 2:84 Autumn 1999
Neil Davidson: The trouble with 'ethnicity' ★ Jim Wolfreys: Class struggles in France ★ Phil Marfleet: Nationalism and internationalism ★ Tom Behan: The return of Italian Communism ★ Andy Durgan: Freedom fighters or Comintern army? The International Brigades in Spain ★ John Molyneux: Art, alienation and capitalism: a reply to Chris Nineham ★ Judy Cox: Dreams of equality: the levelling poor of the English Revolution ★

International Socialism 2:83 Summer 1999
John Rees: The socialist revolution and the democratic revolution ★ Mike Haynes: Theses on the Balkan War ★ Angus Calder: Into slavery: the rise of imperialism ★ Jim Wolfreys: The physiology of barbarism ★ John Newsinger: Scenes from the class war: Ken Loach and socialist cinema ★

International Socialism 2:82 Spring 1999
Lindsey German: The Blair project cracks ★ Dan Atkinson and Larry Elliott: Reflating Keynes: a different view of the crisis ★ Peter Morgan: The new Keynesians: staking a hold in the system? ★ Rob Hoveman: Brenner and crisis: a critique ★ Chris Nineham: Art and alienation: a reply to John Molyneux ★ Paul McGarr: Fascists brought to book ★ Brian Manning: Revisionism revised ★ Neil Davidson: In perspective: Tom Nairn ★

International Socialism 2:81 Winter 1998
Alex Callinicos: World capitalism at the abyss ★ Mike Haynes and Pete Glatter: The Russian catastrophe ★ Phil Marfleet: Globalisation and the Third World ★ Lindsey German: In a class of its own ★ Judy Cox: John Reed: reporting on the revolution ★ Kevin Ovenden: The resistible rise of Adolf Hitler ★

International Socialism 2:80 Autumn 1998
Clare Fermont: Indonesia: the inferno of revolution ★ Workers' representatives and socialists: Three interviews from Indonesia ★ Chris Bambery: Report from Indonesia ★ Tony Cliff: Revolution and counter-revolution: lessons for Indonesia ★ John Molyneux: The legitimacy of modern art ★ Gary McFarlane: A respectable trade? Slavery and the rise of capitalism ★ Paul McGarr: The French Revolution: Marxism versus capitalism ★ Shaun Doherty: Will the real James Connolly please stand up? ★

International Socialism 2:79 Summer 1998
John Rees: The return of Marx? ★ Lindsey German: Reflections on *The Communist Manifesto* ★ Judy Cox: An introduction to Marx's theory of alienation ★ Judith Orr: Making a comeback: the Marxist theory of crisis ★ Megan Trudell: New Labour, old conflicts: the story so far ★ John Molyneux: State of the art ★ Anna Chen: In perspective: Sergei Eisenstein ★ Jonathan Neale: Vietnam veterans ★ Phil Gasper: Bookwatch: Marxism and science ★

International Socialism 2:78 Spring 1998
Colin Sparks: The eye of the storm ★ Shin Gyoung-hee: The crisis and the workers' movement in South Korea ★ Rob Hoveman: Financial crises and the real economy ★ Peter Morgan: Class divisions in the gay community ★ Alex Callinicos: The secret of the dialectic ★ John Parrington: It's life, Jim, but not as we know it ★ Judy Cox: Robin Hood: earl, outlaw or rebel? ★ Ian Birchall: The vice-like hold of nationalism? A comment on Megan Trudell's 'Prelude to revolution' ★ William Keach: In perspective: Alexander Cockburn and Christopher Hitchens ★

International Socialism 2:77 Winter 1997
Audrey Farrell: Addicted to profit—capitalism and drugs ★ Mike Gonzalez: The resurrections of Che Guevara ★ Sam Ashman: India: imperialism, partition and resistance ★ Henry Maitles: Never again! ★ John Baxter: The return of political science ★ Dave Renton: Past its peak ★

International Socialism 2:76 Autumn 1997
Mike Haynes: Was there a parliamentary alternative in 1917? ★ Megan Trudell: Prelude to revolution: class consciousness and the First World War ★ Judy Cox: A light in the darkness ★ Pete Glatter: Victor Serge: writing for the future ★ Gill Hubbard: A guide to action ★ Chris Bambery: Review article: Labour's history of hope and despair ★

International Socialism 2:75 Summer 1997
John Rees: The class struggle under New Labour ★ Alex Callinicos: Europe: the mounting crisis ★ Lance Selfa: Mexico after the Zapatista uprising ★ William Keach: Rise like lions? Shelley and the revolutionary left ★ Judy Cox: What state are we really in? ★ John Parrington: In perspective: Valentin Voloshinov ★

International Socialism 2:74 Spring 1997
Colin Sparks: Tories, Labour and the crisis in education ★ Colin Wilson: The politics of information technology ★ Mike Gonzalez: No more heroes: Nicaragua 1996 ★ Christopher Hill: Tumults and commotions: turning the world upside down ★ Peter Morgan: Capitalism without frontiers? ★ Alex Callinicos: Minds, machines and evolution ★ Anthony Arnove: In perspective: Noam Chomsky ★

International Socialism 2:73 Winter 1996
Chris Harman: Globalisation: a critique of a new orthodoxy ★ Chris Bambery: Marxism and sport ★ John Parrington: Computers and consciousness: a reply to Alex Callinicos ★ Joe Faith: Dennett, materialism and empiricism ★ Megan Trudell: Who made the American Revolution? ★ Mark O'Brien: The class conflicts which shaped British history ★ John Newsinger: From class war to Cold War ★ Alex Callinicos: The state in debate ★ Charlie Kimber: Review article: coming to terms with barbarism in Rwanda in Burundi ★

International Socialism 2:72 Autumn 1996
Alex Callinicos: Betrayal and discontent: Labour under Blair ★ Sue Cockerill and Colin Sparks: Japan in crisis ★ Richard Levins: When science fails us ★ Ian Birchall: The Babeuf bicentenary: conspiracy or revolutionary party? ★ Brian Manning: A voice for the poor ★ Paul O'Flinn: From the kingdom of necessity to the kingdom of freedom: Morris's *News from Nowhere* ★ Clare Fermont: Bookwatch: Palestine and the Middle East 'peace process' ★

International Socialism 2:71 Summer 1996
Chris Harman: The crisis of bourgeois economics ★ Hassan Mahamdallie: William Morris and revolutionary Marxism ★ Alex Callinicos: Darwin, materialism and revolution ★ Chris Nineham: Raymond Williams: revitalising the left? ★ Paul Foot: A passionate prophet of liberation ★ Gill Hubbard: Why has feminism failed women? ★ Lee Sustar: Bookwatch: fighting to unite black and white ★ foreign policy 1945-51 ★ Gareth Jenkins: Novel questions ★ Judy Cox: Blake's revolution ★ Derek Howl: Bookwatch: the Russian Revolution ★

International Socialism 2:70 Spring 1996
Alex Callinicos: South Africa after apartheid ★ Chris Harman: France's hot December ★ Brian Richardson: The making of a revolutionary ★ Gareth Jenkins: Why Lucky Jim turned right—an obituary of Kingsley Amis ★ Mark O'Brien: The bloody birth of capitalism ★ Lee Humber: Studies in revolution ★ Adrian Budd: A new life for Lenin ★ Martin Smith: Bookwatch: the General Strike ★

International Socialism 2:69 Winter 1995
Lindsey German: The Balkan war: can there be peace? ★ Duncan Blackie: The left and the Balkan war ★ Nicolai Gentchev: The myth of welfare dependency ★ Judy Cox: Wealth, poverty and class in Britain today ★ Peter Morgan: Trade unions and strikes ★ Julie Waterson: The party at its peak ★ Megan Trudell: Living to some purpose ★ Nick Howard: The rise and fall of socialism in one city ★ Andy Durgan: Bookwatch: Civil war and revolution in Spain ★

International Socialism 2:68 Autumn 1995
Ruth Brown: Racism and immigration in Britain ★ John Molyneux: Is Marxism deterministic? ★ Stuart Hood: News from nowhere? ★ Lee Sustar: Communism in the heart of the beast ★ Peter Linebaugh: To the teeth and forehead of our faults ★ George Paizis: Back to the future ★ Phil Marshall: The children of stalinism ★ Paul D'Amato: Bookwatch: 100 years of cinema ★

International Socialism 2:67 Summer 1995
Paul Foot: When will the Blair bubble burst? ★ Chris Harman: From Bernstein to Blair—100 years of revisionism ★ Chris Bambery: Was the Second World War a war for democracy? ★ Alex Callinicos: Hope against the Holocaust ★Chris Nineham: Is the media all powerful? ★ Peter Morgan: How the West was won ★ Charlie Hore: Bookwatch: China since Mao ★

International Socialism 2:66 Spring 1995
Dave Crouch: The crisis in Russia and the rise of the right ★ Phil Gasper: Cruel and unusual punishment: the politics of crime in the United States ★ Alex Callinicos: Backwards to liberalism ★ John Newsinger: Matewan: film and working class struggle ★ John Rees: The light and the dark ★ Judy Cox: How to make the Tories disappear ★ Charlie Hore: Jazz: a reply to the critics ★ Pat Riordan: Bookwatch: Ireland ★

International Socialism 2:65 Special issue
Lindsey German: Frederick Engels: life of a revolutionary ★ John Rees: Engels' Marxism ★ Chris Harman: Engels and the origins of human society ★ Paul McGarr: Engels and natural science ★

International Socialism 2:63 Summer 1994
Alex Callinicos: Crisis and class struggle in Europe today ★ Duncan Blackie: The United Nations and the politics of imperialism ★ Brian Manning: The English Revolution and the transition from feudalism to capitalism ★ Lee Sustar: The roots of multi-racial labour unity in the United States ★ Peter Linebaugh: Days of villainy: a reply to two critics ★ Dave Sherry: Trotsky's last, greatest struggle ★ Peter Morgan: Geronimo and the end of the Indian wars ★ Dave Beecham: Ignazio Silone and *Fontamara* ★ Chris Bambery: Bookwatch: understanding fascism ★

International Socialism 2:62 Spring 1994
Sharon Smith: Mistaken identity—or can identity politics liberate the oppressed? ★ Iain Ferguson: Containing the crisis—crime and the Tories ★ John Newsinger: Orwell and the Spanish Revolution ★ Chris Harman: Change at the first millenium ★ Adrian Budd: Nation and empire—Labour's foreign policy 1945-51 ★ Gareth Jenkins: Novel questions ★ Judy Cox: Blake's revolution ★ Derek Howl: Bookwatch: the Russian Revolution ★

International Socialism 2:61 Winter 1994
Lindsey German: Before the flood? ★ John Molyneux: The 'politically correct' controversy ★ David McNally: E P Thompson—class struggle and historical materialism ★ Charlie Hore: Jazz—a people's music ★ Donny Gluckstein: Revolution and the challenge of labour ★ Charlie Kimber: Bookwatch: the Labour Party in decline ★

International Socialism 2:59 Summer 1993
Ann Rogers: Back to the workhouse ★ Kevin Corr and Andy Brown: The labour aristocracy and the roots of reformism ★ Brian Manning: God, Hill and Marx ★ Henry Maitles: Cutting the wire: a criticial appraisal of Primo Levi ★ Hazel Croft: Bookwatch: women and work ★

International Socialism 2:58 Spring 1993

Chris Harman: Where is capitalism going? (part one) ★ Ruth Brown and Peter Morgan: Politics and the class struggle today: a roundtable discussion ★ Richard Greeman: The return of Comrade Tulayev: Victor Serge and the tragic vision of Stalinism ★ Norah Carlin: A new English revolution ★ John Charlton: Building a new world ★ Colin Barker: A reply to Dave McNally ★

International Socialism 2:56 Autumn 1992

Chris Harman: The Return of the National Question ★ Dave Treece: Why the Earth Summit failed ★ Mike Gonzalez: Can Castro survive? ★ Lee Humber and John Rees: The good old cause—an interview with Christopher Hill ★ Ernest Mandel: The Impasse of Schematic Dogmatism ★

International Socialism 2:54 Spring 1992

Sharon Smith: Twilight of the American dream ★ Mike Haynes: Class and crisis—the transition in eastern Europe ★ Costas Kossis: A miracle without end? Japanese capitalism and the world economy ★ Alex Callinicos: Capitalism and the state system: A reply to Nigel Harris ★ Steven Rose: Do animals have rights? ★ John Charlton: Crime and class in the 18th century ★ John Rees: Revolution, reform and working class culture ★ Chris Harman: Blood simple ★

International Socialism 2:51 Summer 1991

Chris Harman: The state and capitalism today ★ Alex Callinicos: The end of nationalism? ★ Sharon Smith: Feminists for a strong state? ★ Colin Sparks and Sue Cockerill: Goodbye to the Swedish miracle ★ Simon Phillips: The South African Communist Party and the South African working class ★ John Brown: Class conflict and the crisis of feudalism ★

International Socialism 2:49 Winter 1990

Chris Bambery: The decline of the Western Communist Parties ★ Ernest Mandel: A theory which has not withstood the test of time ★ Chris Harman: Criticism which does not withstand the test of logic ★ Derek Howl: The law of value In the USSR ★ Terry Eagleton: Shakespeare and the class struggle ★ Lionel Sims: Rape and pre-state societies ★ Sheila McGregor: A reply to Lionel Sims ★

International Socialism 2:48 Autumn 1990

Lindsey German: The last days of Thatcher ★ John Rees: The new imperialism ★ Neil Davidson and Donny Gluckstein: Nationalism and the class struggle in Scotland ★ Paul McGarr: Order out of chaos ★

International Socialism 2:44 Autumn 1989

Charlie Hore: China: Tiananmen Square and after ★ Sue Clegg: Thatcher and the welfare state ★ John Molyneux: *Animal Farm* revisited ★ David Finkel: After Arias, is the revolution over? ★ John Rose: Jews in Poland ★

International Socialism 2:18 Winter 1983

Donny Gluckstein: Workers' councils in Western Europe ★ Jane Ure Smith: The early Communist press in Britain ★ John Newsinger: The Bolivian Revolution ★ Andy Durgan: Largo Caballero and Spanish socialism ★ M Barker and A Beezer: Scarman and the language of racism ★

International Socialism 2:14 Winter 1981

Chris Harman: The riots of 1981 ★ Dave Beecham: Class struggle under the Tories ★ Tony Cliff: Alexandra Kollontai ★ L James and A Paczuska: Socialism needs feminism ★ Reply to Cliff on Zetkin ★ Feminists In the labour movement ★